Easy Recipes
for the
Traveling Cook

by **Ferne Holmes**

Golden West Publishers

Cover design by Bruce Robert Fischer

Artwork by Ferne Holmes

Library of Congress Cataloging-in-Publication Data

Holmes, Ferne
    Easy recipes for the traveling cook.

    Includes index.
    1. Cookery. 2. Mobile home living. I. Title.
TX840.M6H65 1987   641.5'75   87-8565
ISBN 0-914-84629-9 (pbk.)

Printed in the United States of America

Information in this book is deemed to be authentic and accurate by author and publisher. However, they disclaim any liability incurred in connection with the use of information appearing in this book.

Golden West Publishers
4113 N. Longview Ave.
Phoenix, AZ 85014. USA

Dedication

A special thanks to husband, John, who sat on the edge of distant mountains and the sands of remote beaches bravely eating the failures as well as the successes that led to this book.

I salute you, John. You are an honest "food tester"!

Thanks also to my two Moms, Aagot Sheetz of Norfolk, Virginia, and Dorothy Holmes of Moorhead, Minnesota, for sharing family recipes and offering words of encouragement.

Contents

Introduction

We could have called this book the "I Never Missed a Sunset Cook Book."

Why? you ask. The answer is simple. The recipes are easily prepared and take little cooking time. So, unlike many traveling cooks, I never miss a sunset!

It is obvious as we visit parks and campgrounds throughout the United States and Mexico that more Americans are on the road than ever before. All of the traveling cooks share the common problem of what to make for dinner: something that is easy, quick to prepare and different.

Many years ago, guilt pushed me into revising old recipes and trying new ideas using canned meats. I felt guilty when I just opened a can of beans or stew.

Many of our recipes use canned meats because we enjoy visiting remote areas located far from grocery stores. We have found many "full timers," campers and vacationers who enjoy distant horizons as much as we do and they, too, worry about what to do with canned foods.

All of our recipes have been used many times during our fifteen years of outdoor living.

We hope you will enjoy using our book as much as we enjoyed writing it!

Ferne Holmes

Preparation

Whether you cook over a campfire, on a portable gas stove or in a camper, trailer or motor home, you will need some kind of cooking equipment. Our suggestions may be used as a check list.

Your needs will be determined by the number of people you cook for and the type of cooking you will be doing.

Equipment Suggestions

Saucepans & Skillets

Sizes I use most frequently are one-half quart, one quart and three quart. The pans should have covers. Teflon-coated pans make cooking and cleaning easier.

Two skillets I must have, wherever I do my cooking, are the 8- and 10-inch size. Both have covers and are Teflon-coated.

We also have a round, Teflon-coated roaster. It is used as a salad bowl for campground pot lucks, a soup tureen, and on occasion, a roaster.

Our cooking utensils are stored on their sides in a homemade rack under the sink. Each utensil has its own slot in the rack. This protects the Teflon coating and does not take up much space.

There is still room for soaps, foil, plastic wrap, garbage bags, bread board, bug spray, window cleaner and various other small items. The dishpan, tea kettle and flat toaster also fit there.

Baking Pans

The 8x8", 9x9" and 9x13" are handy sizes. We use aluminum pans and also have a two-quart casserole. Of course, you don't need these if you will not be baking. We also carry a cookie sheet that doubles as a tray.

Storage Bowls

Plastic bowls that may be nested are most convenient. Save your margarine, and non-dairy whip bowls and covers.

Tea Kettle, Coffee Pot

If you use instant coffee, all you need is a tea kettle.

Stove Top Toaster

Camp supply stores have a flat, square toaster with a handle. It is metal with screen on one side and small holes on the other side. It will hold four slices of bread and is used over one burner. It is perfect for heating rolls or tortillas wrapped in foil and may be stored on its side (fits into storage space under the sink).

Dishes & Utensils

Plates, cups, bowls and glasses, preferably plastic. The 8-ounce "throw away" glasses are nice for dessert cups. They may be washed and reused several times before they crack. If you use paper plates, plastic or basket plate holders will make them sturdier.

Stainless steel flatware, can opener, measuring cups and spoons, potato peeler, sharp knives, large spoons and forks for cooking purposes, spatula, tongs, egg beater, pastry brush, cork screw and salt and pepper shakers.

Other Kitchen Items

Dish pan, strainer, dish towels, dish cloths, hand towels, toothpicks, matches, hot pads, fly swatter, soap dish, plastic tablecloth (or placemats) and a flashlight.

Plastic Storage Bags, Garbage Bags and Plastic Wrap

Heavy Duty Aluminum Foil

Aluminum Foil Pans

These pans are available in grocery stores. If you do not want to carry aluminum baking pans or casserole dishes, these "throw away" pans will be useful.

Paper Towels and Facial Tissue

First Aid Kit

Campfire Cooking

(See the campfire cooking section of the book.)

Final Suggestion

We have listed the things we use on our trips. It is wise to make out your personal check list and then use it before you leave on a trip. Anything, other than the first aid kit not used after the first two or three trips, can probably be left at home.

If you haven't used the first aid kit, you must be doing something right! Be sure to check your medical supplies periodically and replace outdated medication or things in short supply.

Hints for Traveling Cooks

Planning ahead makes mealtime easier, whether you are at home or camping. Some of the ways to plan ahead for camping trips are as follows:

Before leaving home, pre-cook five or six potatoes. They can be used for hash, hash browns or potato salad. Bake a roast beef and slice part of it for sandwiches and shred the rest to be used in a variety of dishes. Cook a pound or two of chorizo (Mexican sausage) or bulk sausage. It makes breakfast a snap! Chicken may be cooked and boned for salads, sandwiches or a variety of hot dishes. Freeze the cooked meats in serving-size packages. Use plastic freezing bags or the plastic wrap you seal yourself. Pack the packages so they will be flat and you can get more into the RV freezer. The amount you cook ahead depends on your freezer size.

When camping, if you are going to cook fresh meat, use larger cuts of meat so you will have leftovers. For example:

- Family-style pork ribs for one meal: the leftover meat can be shredded for barbecued sandwiches, diced for chow mein or made into sweet and sour pork.
- Stove top roast beef for dinner: you may want to shred leftovers for machaca beef or tacos.
- Leftover chicken: heat in a can of soup and serve with dumplings.
- Choose your cooking time. If it is a rainy day and you are inside reading, boil potatoes or eggs to be used for quick meals when the sun is shining. Have the day you are writing letters be the day you fix the roast or chicken.
- If you will be staying at a campground or park where electricity is available, be sure to take along an electric fry pan. Whole meals may be prepared in them. You can even heat rolls by wrapping them in foil and placing the package on top of what you are cooking, and covering the pan. Include an extension cord (if the weather is nice) so you can use the electric fry pan to cook outside.
- Non-dairy milk substitutes taste like cream on breakfast cereal and keep longer than milk. Some areas have sterile milk in cartons (do not require refrigeration until opened). When cold, it tastes the same as fresh milk and may be used in pudding mixes and other dishes successfully.
- Crackers, rusks, melba toast, bread sticks, etc., take the place of bread and do not get stale.

- Most RV's and campers have storage space under the dinette seats. It is handy to have a cardboard box that will fit that area. Use the box for your canned supplies and you will find it easy to pull the box out to find what you need. When stowing supplies, sort the cans either into meal order (putting the ones to be used toward the end of your trip in the back of the box) or put them in rows of vegetables, meats, soups, etc. If you have room in your refrigerator, store some of your canned fruits there.
- A large round or square tin box with a tight cover is great for crackers. Mine holds close to three boxes of crackers, so we always have an assortment to choose from. Fill the tin box before you leave home.
- Sugar, flour, instant tea and coffee are easy to get to and take up less space in the cupboard when stored in plastic pint or quart containers.
- If you do not have a refrigerator you can still take some frozen foods along. Use one of the heavy plastic insulated coolers with an attached cover. Put in a block of ice, placing it in one side of the chest. If the block of ice covers more than half the ice chest, chip off the extra ice. Leave chipped ice in bottom of the chest and stack packages of frozen meats, etc., on top. Fill the chest completely with crushed ice. Be sure it gets into all crevices. Lay a flat package of dry ice on top, latch the cover securely and tape with silver duct tape all the way around the lid. Open the drain once in awhile so water may drain out. Keep the chest out of direct sun. Meat has stayed frozen for over two weeks for us when packed this way.

Menus

	BREAKFAST	**LUNCH	DINNER

FIRST DAY	Orange Wedges
	*Cinnamon
	  French Toast
	Syrup
	Bacon
	Beverage
		Instant Soup
		Lunch Meat
		  Sandwiches
		Banana
		Beverage
			*Campfire Steak
			*Potato-Onion Bake
			*Italian Garden
			  Salad
			*Peanut Butter
			  Surprise Cookies
			Beverage

SECOND DAY	Juice
	Cereal
	Toast & Jam
	Beverage
		*Ole Hamburger
		  Salad
		Tortilla Chips
		Beverage
			*Crusty Crab Cakes
			  with *Zesty
			  Mustard Sauce
			Hash Brown Potatoes
			*Company Green
			  Beans
			*Fruit Slush
			Beverage

THIRD DAY	Juice
	*Mexican Roll-ups
	Beverage
		Instant Soup
		Lunch Meat
		  Sandwich
		Apple
		Beverage
			*Campfire Chili Stew
			Lettuce & Italian
			  Dressing
			*Fudgy Graham
			  Cracker Cookies
			Beverage

FOURTH DAY	Orange Wedges
	Pancakes (use
	  baking mix)
	Bacon
	Syrup
	Beverage
		*Shrimp Salad
		(see Fresh Fish
		  Salad)
		Crackers &
		  Cheese Spread
		Cookies
		Beverage
			*Chicken &
			  Dumplings
			*Gingered Carrots
			*Caramel Apple Cake
			Beverage

FIFTH DAY	Juice
	*Easy Spanish
	  Omelet
	Toast or Rusks
	Beverage
		*Macaroni Tuna
		  Salad
		Crackers &
		  Cheese
		Beverage
			*Ham & Scalloped
			  Potatoes
			*Pineapple Slaw
			Applesauce
			Angel Food Cake
			Beverage

SIXTH DAY	Juice
	*Cereal &
	  Applesauce
	  (See cold
	  cereal treats)
	Cinnamon Toast
	Beverage
		Instant Soup
		Grilled Cheese
		  Sandwich
		Cookies
		Beverage
			*Roast Beef Hash
			Sliced Tomatoes,
			  Carrot Sticks &
			  Celery
			*Butterscotch Pudding
			Beverage

SEVENTH DAY	½ Grapefruit
	*Hearty Scramble
	Toast or Rusks
	Beverage
		Corn Beef
		  Sandwich
		  (chill beef
		  before slicing)
		Tortilla Chips
		  & Salsa
		Beverage
			*Ham On A Stick
			*Potatoes In A Pouch
			Fresh Vegetables with
			  *Hot Cheese Dip
			  (use all the rest of
			  the fresh vegetables,
			  carrots, cauliflower,
			  celery, zucchini,
			  radishes)
			*Roasted Caramel
			  Apples
			Beverage

*RECIPES GIVEN IN BOOK
**Lunches may not be hearty enough for your family. If they aren't, have extra chips, canned fruits or cookies to round out the meal.

Stocking the Cupboard

(Ingredients listed are adequate for two persons
with hearty appetites for two weeks of travel.)

2 grapefruit
8 apples
6 bananas
2 lemons
10 oranges
1 small cabbage
1 head lettuce
1 package carrots
1 cauliflower
3 bags of radishes
8 medium potatoes
1 small onion
4 small-to-medium zucchini
9 plum or Italian tomatoes
1 (16-oz.) can stewed tomatoes
2 (16-oz.) cans small whole white
    potatoes
1 (16-oz.) can cut green beans
1 (16-oz.) can small whole carrots
1 (4-oz.) can whole mushrooms
1 (2.5-oz.) can French-fried
    onion rings
2 cans applesauce
1 can apple pie mix
1 (8½-oz.) can crushed pineapple
1 (16-oz.) can mixed vegetables
1 small can orange slices
1½ to 2-inch thick steak for four
1 lb. lean ground beef
1 cup cooked chorizo
    (cook at home and freeze)
1 lb. bacon
Luncheon meat
    (enough for two lunches)
1 jar bacon bits
3 (6.5-oz.) cans crab meat
3 (5- to 6-oz.) cans shrimp

2 (7½-oz.) cans tuna
2 (12-oz.) cans corn beef
1 (9¼-oz.) can tuna
3 (12-oz.) cans roast beef
    and gravy
2 (10- to 12-oz.) cans chicken
3 (one-lb.) canned hams
3 boxes hash brown potatoes
2 boxes au gratin potatoes
1 box macaroni
1 (medium size) box buttermilk
    baking mix
1 box graham crackers
1 box vanilla wafers
1 bag cookies (any kind)
Assorted crackers
    (include soda crackers)
1 box rusks (replaces toast if you
    run short of bread)
1 angel food loaf cake
Tortilla chips
8 small flour tortillas
3 large loaves of bread
2 jars caramel ice cream topping
1 jar dry roasted peanuts
1 can ready-made fudge frosting
1 jar peanut butter
1 jar jam
1 large bag marshmallows
2 cans cream of chicken soup
Instant soup mix
    (enough for 3 lunches)
1 box vanilla instant pudding
4 cans evaporated milk
2 large cans fruit juice
    for breakfasts
1 large jar salsa

1 bottle catsup
1 jar mustard
1 quart mayonnaise
1 small bottle Worcestershire sauce
1 small bottle lemon juice
1 small bottle vinegar
1 small jar horseradish
1 bottle (Italian-style)
    salad dressing
1 bottle olive oil or vegetable oil
1 large container maple syrup
Cold cereal
    (enough for 2 breakfasts)
4 quarts milk (3 frozen in freezer)
1 quart non-dairy creamer
    for cereal
1 dozen eggs
3 cartons egg substitute
    (each carton equivalent
    to 2 eggs)
1 (12- or 16-oz.) package
    cheese slices
1 small package shredded
    cheddar cheese

1 lb. box cheese (kind that
    does not require
    refrigeration until opened)
1 jar soft cheese spread (large size)
2 lbs. margarine or butter
1 can ground powdered mustard
1 can celery seeds
1 can celery flakes
1 can dried parsley
1 can dried onion (minced)
1 can chili powder
1 bottle garlic powder
Salt and pepper
1 can cinnamon
1 can powdered ginger
1 can paprika
1 (1¼-oz.) package taco seasoning
1 jar instant chicken bouillon
Brown sugar, white sugar, flour
Cornstarch
Instant tea, coffee, cocoa,
    beverages

You will need small amounts of sugar, brown sugar, flour and cornstarch. After you check the recipes, take along just what you would use. Cleaning fresh vegetables at home and packing them in plastic bags also will save space in the refrigerator.

Some of the spices and other things that are a must for this traveling cook include:

- Basil
- Buttermilk baking mix
- Canned milk
- Catsup and prepared mustard
- Celery flakes
- Celery seed
- Chili powder
- Cinnamon
- Cooking oil and olive oil
- Cornstarch
- Dill weed
- Dried minced onion
- Dried parsley
- Egg substitute
- Flour
- Ginger
- Ground mustard
- Instant beef and chicken bouillon
- Lemon or lime juice
- Nutmeg
- Oregano
- Pepper
- Powdered garlic
- Salsa
- Salt
- Seasoned salt
- Soy sauce
- Sugar (white and brown)
- Tabasco
- Vinegar
- Worcestershire sauce

Pre-Travel Food Planning

Prior to your trip, it is a good idea to give some thought to what you will be cooking. Look at the recipes you plan to use so that you will have the supplies you need.

How you stock your camp kitchen is largely determined by the type of vacation you are taking and the number of people you will be cooking for. If you are going to be in a remote area, you will need more canned goods. If you will be in an RV park where supplies are available, you will probably be using less canned foods. Always carry enough food to get you by in case of an emergency.

The menus in this book are for one week of wilderness camping. Extras include baking mix for pancakes or biscuits, cheeses, crackers and canned meats.

Plan to use fresh meat the first part of your trip. After you have planned a one-week menu, it is easy to add to your grocery list for the second week. We store two cartons of egg substitute, chicken breasts and one pound of hamburger in our freezer for the second week. We also carry an extra can of roast beef, corn beef, chicken, ham, tuna, a jar of processed cheese spread and a one-pound box of processed cheese.

In addition to those items, we take a large box of buttermilk baking mix, instant rice, instant potato buds, hash browns, scalloped potatoes and macaroni. For vegetables, corn, beans, green beans and tomatoes add to a variety of dishes. Three or four cans of salsa and evaporated milk are also useful.

These extra supplies are enough for a second week. More than once we have been unable to leave a remote area due to heavy rain or higher-than-normal tides. Our extra supplies enabled us to sit back and enjoy our extended vacation.

Recipe Notes

Something Good for Breakfast

Sunrise breakfast, a late brunch or breakfast on the run; this section contains recipes to fit all occasions.

French Toast

4 EGGS (beaten)
¼ cup MILK (fresh or canned)
2 Tbsp. SUGAR
1 Tbsp. ground CINNAMON
8 slices FRENCH BREAD (or any bread)
2 to 3 Tbsp. MARGARINE (or cooking oil)

Combine first four ingredients in a shallow pan and mix well. Trim bread crusts, if desired. Melt margarine in a fry pan. Dip bread in the egg mixture and fry until golden brown on both sides. Serve with a dusting of powdered sugar and a side of applesauce or maple syrup.

Sausage Pancakes

PANCAKE MIX (or buttermilk baking mix)
½ lb. bulk SAUSAGE
2 to 3 Tbsp. MARGARINE (or cooking oil)

Prepare pancake batter for four, according to instructions on package. Brown and crumble sausage. Drain off all grease and add sausage to pancake batter. Mix thoroughly. Melt margarine on griddle and fry pancakes. Serve with hot raspberry or blackberry jam. Melt jam over low heat, adding water a tablespoon at a time until it reaches desired consistency.

Applesauce Pancakes

1 cup APPLESAUCE
1 EGG (beaten)
1/3 cup MILK
2 Tbsp. SUGAR
1 tsp. ground CINNAMON (optional)
1 cup BUTTERMILK BAKING MIX
2 to 3 Tbsp. MARGARINE (or cooking oil)

Combine all ingredients except margarine and mix well. Melt margarine on griddle and fry pancakes on one side until surface is bubbly. Turn and brown other side. If you have a Teflon-coated griddle, you need very little margarine. Serve with maple syrup. (Makes 10 to 12 pancakes)

Sunday Brunch Eggs & Cheese Sauce

4 EGGS
3 Tbsp. MILK
¼ tsp. PEPPER
1 Tbsp. MARGARINE
4 slices HAM (or 8 strips crisp bacon)
4 ENGLISH MUFFINS (toasted)
SALSA (optional)

Combine first three ingredients and beat until foamy. Melt margarine in fry pan and scramble eggs to soft set. Make four servings by placing two muffin halves on a plate; place ham or bacon on top of muffins and one-quarter of the egg mixture on top of the breakfast meat. Top with 2 or 3 Tbsp. Cheese Sauce.*

*CHEESE SAUCE

½ lb. VELVEETA CHEESE
½ cup MILK (fresh or canned)
1½ tsp. CORNSTARCH

Over low heat, melt cheese and one-quarter cup milk. Mix cornstarch with rest of milk. When the cheese is completely melted, add cornstarch mixture to cheese. Stir constantly while mixture thickens slightly. If mixture gets too thick, add additional milk a spoonful at a time until desired consistency is reached.

Mexican Eggs

¼ cup WATER
1½ cups CHUNKY SALSA
4 EGGS

Combine water and salsa in a fry pan and stir to mix. Heat until salsa starts to bubble. Break eggs into pan. Turn heat down and cover pan. Cook until eggs are done the way you like them. Baste once or twice during cooking time. Serve with warm tortillas and refried beans.

Breakfast Pie

2 cups cooked or canned HAM (diced)
1 cup CHEDDAR CHEESE (shredded)
1½ cups MILK (fresh or canned)
¾ cup BUTTERMILK BAKING MIX
3 EGGS (slightly beaten)
1 tsp. CELERY FLAKES
¼ cup SALSA

Spread ham evenly in bottom of greased 9 or 10-inch pie pan. Sprinkle with one-half cup cheese. Combine next four ingredients and mix well. Pour over ham and cheese. Spoon salsa over top of pie; sprinkle with rest of cheese and bake at 400 degrees for 35 minutes (or until knife inserted into middle of the pie comes out clean). (4 to 6 servings)

Hearty Scramble

3 Tbsp. MARGARINE
1 cup cooked or canned POTATOES (diced)
3 EGGS (beaten)
3 Tbsp. MILK
1 tsp. CELERY SEED
1 Tbsp. DRIED ONION (minced or chopped)
¼ cup BACON BITS

Melt margarine in fry pan and lightly brown potatoes. Beat eggs with milk, celery seed and onion. Pour over potatoes. Add bacon bits. Stir to mix and scramble. (Serves 4)

Devil's Sandwich

2 Tbsp. MARGARINE
4 EGGS
4 slices TOAST
1 can (2¼-oz.) DEVILED HAM

Melt margarine in fry pan and fry eggs, over easy or sunny side up.
Spread each slice of toast with one-quarter of the deviled ham. Put
egg on top of toast and serve with Mexican Cheese Sauce.* May serve
additional toast on the side.

*MEXICAN CHEESE SAUCE

1 tsp. CORNSTARCH
½ cup mild to hot CHUNKY SALSA
½ lb. VELVEETA CHEESE

Mix cornstarch into the salsa. Melt cheese over low heat; add salsa
and stir until thoroughly blended and slightly thickened.

Bacon & Egg
Breakfast Sandwich

4 EGGS (beaten)
3 Tbsp. MILK
1 tsp. DRIED ONION (minced or chopped)
¼ tsp. CELERY SEED
¼ tsp. PEPPER
¼ tsp. SALT
½ cup BACON BITS
1 Tbsp. MARGARINE

Beat together first six ingredients. Melt margarine in 8-inch fry pan.
Pour eggs into hot fry pan, sprinkle with bacon bits and cook over
medium heat until center of the mixture is almost set. Loosen eggs
from the side of the pan and turn over to brown other side. Divide
eggs into four servings and make sandwich using toast or bread.

Mexican Roll-Ups

4 EGGS
2 Tbsp. WATER
½ cup cooked CHORIZO* (well drained)
1 Tbsp. MARGARINE
8 Tbsp. soft CHEESE SPREAD (comes in a jar)
8 FLOUR TORTILLAS (small size, warmed)**

Beat eggs and water together. Add cooked chorizo. Melt margarine in a fry pan and scramble eggs to soft set. Spread one tablespoon cheese on each warm tortilla. Put one-eighth of egg mixture down the center of each tortilla and turn up opposite ends of tortilla to help hold mixture in. Then roll tortilla from one of the unfolded sides. Serve hot. (4 servings)

* Cook chorizo at home and drain thoroughly. Freeze flat in freezer bags by the one-half cup. Easy to carry in your RV freezer.

** To warm tortillas, wrap the number you need in aluminum foil. Lay the packet over a very low flame for one or two minutes on each side. If you have a kettle of hot water or a hot coffee pot, set the packet to one side and put the hot pot on top of it. The tortillas will stay warm until you need them.

Easy Spanish Omelet

1 EGG
1 Tbsp. MILK
½ tsp. DRIED ONION (minced or chopped)
1 Tbsp. MARGARINE
2 Tbsp. SALSA
half of a processed CHEESE SLICE

Beat egg, milk and onion together. Melt margarine in a fry pan and pour in egg. Cook over medium heat until almost set (tip pan so uncooked egg runs to the sides and cooks). Put salsa on one-half of the omelet and add cheese on top of salsa. Fold other half of the omelet over the filling; cover and cook one minute or until cheese melts. (1 serving)

Baked Eggs

1 can (10¾-oz.) CHEDDAR CHEESE SOUP
¾ cup MILK
5 EGGS (beaten)
¼ cup BACON BITS
PAPRIKA

Combine first three ingredients and mix well. Pour into a greased 9-inch pie pan. Sprinkle on bacon bits and paprika. Bake at 375 degrees for about 45 minutes or until knife inserted in the middle comes out clean. Good served on toast or with warm tortillas and chunky salsa. (4 to 6 servings)

Breakfast Beans

¼ cup MILK (fresh or canned)
1 can (16-oz.) REFRIED BEANS
2 Tbsp. hot SALSA
½ cup CHEDDAR CHEESE (shredded)

Combine first three ingredients in a saucepan and mix well. Heat over medium flame for about 10 minutes. Stir; sprinkle with cheese and cover pan. Turn off heat and let beans sit for a few minutes so cheese starts to melt. (4 servings)

Creamed Ham & Eggs

2½ cups MILK
3½ Tbsp. FLOUR
½ tsp. PEPPER
1 can (4-oz.) mild CHILIES (diced)
2 Tbsp. MARGARINE
4 EGGS (hard boiled and cut into 8 pieces each)
1 cup cooked or canned HAM (diced)

Combine one-half cup of milk and the flour in a saucepan and stir until smooth. Slowly stir in rest of milk. Add pepper, chilies and margarine and heat over a low flame until mixture starts to thicken. Add cut up eggs and ham and stir in so they are covered with the sauce. Continue to heat over low flame for five minutes or until eggs and ham are hot. Serve on toast or toasted English muffins. (Serves 4)

Cold Cereal Treats

1 cup RICE CEREAL
¼ to ½ cup YOGURT (orange, lemon or strawberry)
2 Tbsp. SUNFLOWER SEED KERNELS

1 cup GRANOLA CEREAL
½ cup APPLESAUCE

1 cup GRANOLA CEREAL
½ cup APPLESAUCE
¼ cup YOGURT (plain)

In each instance, mix the cup of cereal with the listed ingredients and eat at once.

Appetizers

"Nippy Shrimp Toast" or "Hot Cheese Dip" served with chips or crackers and your favorite beverage are perfect for the "watching the sunset" bunch!

Nippy Shrimp Toast

1 can (5-oz.) small SHRIMP (drained)
½ cup MAYONNAISE
1 tsp. GROUND MUSTARD
¼ cup CHEDDAR CHEESE (grated)
6 slices BREAD (crusts removed)

Mash shrimp and combine all ingredients in a bowl and mix well. Toast bread on one side (in the broiler). Spread one-sixth shrimp mixture on untoasted side of the bread. Cut each slice of bread into four pieces and place under the broiler until mixture is bubbly and lightly browned. Serve hot. (Makes 24 squares)

Steamed Clams

Scrub fresh clams and purge by putting in a bucket of water (fresh or salt) for two hours. Purge before steaming.

There are two methods for steaming clams that have worked well for us.

FIRST METHOD: Place scrubbed clams in a large pot and cover with boiling water. Cover pot and let sit for 15 minutes. *Only use the clams that have opened. Discard the others.* This method works well on the smaller clams.

SECOND METHOD: Place scrubbed clams in a large pot and cover with water. Bring to a boil and cook for two to three minutes or until shells start to open. Remove from heat, cover and let sit for about 15 minutes. *Discard any clams that do not open.* This is the method we normally use for the larger clams.

Steamed clams are an outdoor appetizer. Serve in the shell with Lemon Butter*. Have a bucket (handy for discarded shells) and small forks or toothpicks for holding the clams when dipping in sauce.

*LEMON BUTTER

1 cup BUTTER (or margarine)
2 Tbsp. LEMON JUICE
2 to 3 drops TABASCO (or hot sauce, optional)

Combine ingredients in a small pan and heat until butter is melted and hot.

Creamy Clam Dip

2 pkg. (3-oz.) CREAM CHEESE (softened)
¼ cup MILK
½ cup MAYONNAISE
1 Tbsp. LEMON JUICE
1 Tbsp. DRIED PARSLEY
½ tsp. GROUND MUSTARD
1 can (6½-oz.) CLAMS & JUICE (chopped or minced)

Combine first six ingredients and mix until soft and smooth and thoroughly mixed. Add clams and juice and mix well. Chill before serving. Serve with crackers.

Chili Crab Dip

2 pkgs. (3-oz. each) CREAM CHEESE (softened)
¼ cup CHILI SAUCE
½ cup MAYONNAISE
½ tsp. GROUND MUSTARD
1 can (6.5 oz.) CRAB MEAT

Combine first four ingredients and mix until soft and smooth and thoroughly mixed. Flake crab into mixture (checking for shell bits or membrane as you flake). Mix well and chill before serving with crackers.

Crab Cocktail

1 cup shredded LETTUCE
½ cup CATSUP
½ Tbsp. HORSERADISH
1 Tbsp. LEMON JUICE
1 can (6.5-oz.) CRAB MEAT (flaked)

Make a nest of one-half cup lettuce in two bowls. Combine catsup, horseradish and lemon juice. Add flaked crab (check for shell bits as you flake it). Mix and place one-half on each lettuce nest. (Serves 2)

Shrimp Dip

2 cartons (8-oz.) plain YOGURT
1 tsp. INSTANT CHICKEN BOUILLON
½ tsp. GROUND MUSTARD
2 Tbsp. ONION SOUP MIX
1 can (5-oz.) small SHRIMP (drained)

Combine first four ingredients and mix well. Mash shrimp and add to yogurt mixture, mix thoroughly. Chill for one to two hours before serving. Serve with crackers or chips.

Ceviche
(Raw Fish In Lime Juice)

2½ to 3 cups RAW FISH (boned & cut into small pieces)
½ cup LIME JUICE (fresh if possible)

Place fish in a shallow container and add lime juice. Push fish around so each piece is covered. If juice does not cover fish, add two to three tablespoons of water. Cover and refrigerate for about two hours. Stir fish around twice during this time. Lime juice will "cook" fish. The fish will be white and appear cooked when it is ready. Squeeze out juice, rinse with water and squeeze out water. Place fish in a bowl and cover with Salsa*.

*SALSA

1½ cups chunky SALSA (medium to hot)
1 small ONION (minced)
2 TOMATOES (chopped)
¼ cup OLIVE OIL
2 Tbsp. LIME JUICE

Combine all ingredients and pour over fish. Let chill for one to two hours before serving with crackers.

Quick Guacamole Dip

3 large ripe AVOCADOS (peeled & mashed)
2 Tbsp. LEMON JUICE (or lime juice)
½ cup MAYONNAISE
¼ cup chunky SALSA (mild to hot)

Mash avocados, add all ingredients and mix well. Serve with tortilla chips.

Mexican Bean & Cheese Dip

1 can (8-oz.) REFRIED BEANS
¼ cup MILK
½ cup chunky SALSA (hot)
½ lb. VELVEETA CHEESE

Combine beans, milk and salsa in a small pan and mix well. Heat over low flame while you cut cheese into small chunks and add it to beans. Stir as mixture heats and cheese melts. When cheese is completely melted, serve hot with chips.

Salmon Party Ball

1 can (16-oz.) SALMON (drained)
1 pkg. (8-oz.) CREAM CHEESE (softened)
1 Tbsp. LEMON JUICE
1 Tbsp. DRIED ONION (minced or chopped)
1 tsp. GROUND MUSTARD
1 Tbsp. DRIED PARSLEY
½ cup PECANS (finely-chopped)

Flake salmon into a bowl. Remove skin and bone and discard. Mash cheese and lemon juice until cheese is smooth and soft. Mash into the flaked salmon. Add onion, mustard and parsley and mix well. Shape into a ball and roll in the nuts. Wrap and refrigerate for several hours or over night. Serve with crackers.

Peppered Vienna Sausages

1 cup JALAPENO PEPPER JELLY
2 Tbsp. WATER
2 can (5-oz.) VIENNA SAUSAGES (drained)

Melt jelly and water in a small pan. Cut Vienna sausages in half and add to sauce. Spoon sauce over sausages and continue to heat over low flame until sausages are hot. (If jelly is not available, mint jelly with one to two drops of hot sauce may be substituted.) Serve sausages hot with toothpicks for spearing.

Hot Cheese Dip

¾ cup chunky SALSA (hot)
1 lb. VELVEETA CHEESE

Heat salsa in a pan. Cut cheese into pieces and add to salsa. Stir as cheese melts. When cheese is melted, let dip sit for three or four minutes. Stir and serve with chips or fresh raw vegetables (cauliflower, zucchini, radishes, etc.).

Cream Cheese & Chili Spread

1 pkg. (8-oz.) CREAM CHEESE (softened)
2 Tbsp. MILK
1 tsp. CELERY SEED (optional)
½ cup CHILI SAUCE

Mash first three ingredients together until smooth. Add chili sauce and mix well. Serve with tortilla chips or crackers.

Ripe Olive Roll-Ups

¾ cup ripe black OLIVES (chopped)
¼ cup PECANS (or walnuts, finely-chopped)
3 to 4 Tbsp. MAYONNAISE
12 slices white BREAD (crusts removed)

Combine olives and nuts in a bowl and add mayonnaise a spoonful at a time and mix well. Use just enough mayonnaise to hold nuts and olives together. Spread about a tablespoon of the mixture on each slice of bread and roll up and secure with a toothpick. Toast under broiler until lightly browned. Serve hot.

Marinated Mushrooms

16 to 20 large fresh MUSHROOMS (cleaned)
Italian-style SALAD DRESSING

Place mushrooms in a bowl and cover with dressing. Place a small plate on top to hold them under the dressing. Refrigerate for two to three hours.

Ham & Cheese Roll-Ups

1 pkg. (3-oz.) CREAM CHEESE
1 Tbsp. MILK
¼ tsp. CELERY SEED
3 Tbsp. green stuffed OLIVES (chopped)
12 slices HAM LUNCH MEAT (thin slices)

Mash first three ingredients together until cheese is soft and smooth. Add olives and mix well. Spread the 12 ham slices with cheese mixture and roll tightly. Cut in half and chill before serving on crackers.

Recipe Notes

_____

_____

_____

_____

_____

_____

_____

_____

_____

_____

_____

_____

_____

_____

_____

_____

_____

_____

_____

_____

_____

_____

_____

Salads and Salad Dressings

Many "full time" RVers stay in one spot for extended periods. They plant small vegetable plots near their homes on wheels. Even in Mexico we found the sun followers enjoying home-grown tomatoes, leaf lettuce, cucumbers and snap beans.

Old Fashioned Cole Slaw

3 cups CABBAGE (finely-chopped)
½ cup cider VINEGAR
3 Tbsp. OLIVE OIL
3 Tbsp. SUGAR
3 Tbsp. WATER
1 Tbsp. DRIED ONION (minced or chopped)
1 tsp. CELERY SEED
½ tsp. GROUND MUSTARD

Chop cabbage and put aside. Combine rest of ingredients in a pint jar and shake to mix. Pour over cabbage and refrigerate for one to two hours before serving. Stir well and serve. (Yield: 3 cups)

Layered Salad

2½ cups LETTUCE (shredded)
½ lb. canned HAM (diced)
2 small ZUCCHINI (sliced thin)
1 can (5- to 7-oz.) CHICKEN (drained and flaked)
3 small TOMATOES (chopped)
1 jar (6½-oz.) ARTICHOKE HEARTS (cut up)
1 can (2.5-oz.) FRENCH-FRIED ONION RINGS

A "see through" bowl is nice for this salad, but is not essential. Layer the first five ingredients in a bowl in order given. When artichoke hearts and juice are added, use a fork to help juice work through the layers. Add onion ring layer and serve with or without salad dressing. Buttermilk Salad Dressing* or French Dressing** are both excellent on this salad. (Serves 4 to 6)

*BUTTERMILK SALAD DRESSING

1 cup MAYONNAISE
1 Tbsp. DRIED PARSLEY
1 to 1½ tsp. GARLIC POWDER (to taste)
½ tsp. PEPPER
1 tsp. CELERY SEED
½ tsp. SALT
BUTTERMILK (about 1 cup)

Put mayonnaise in a pint jar and add the next five items. Stir to mix and add buttermilk, leaving enough room at the top of the jar to be able to shake contents (not quite a cup). Shake vigorously to mix. Dressing keeps well when refrigerated. (Yield: 1 pint)

**FRENCH DRESSING

1 cup SUGAR
1 cup cider VINEGAR
1 cup VEGETABLE OIL
1 can (small) TOMATO PASTE
3 Tbsp. DRIED ONION (minced or chopped)
2 Tbsp. DRIED PARSLEY
1 tsp. CELERY SEED

Combine all ingredients in a large jar and shake to mix. Refrigerate for two or more hours before using. (About 2 cups)

Pineapple Cole Slaw

4 cups CABBAGE (finely-chopped)

Chop cabbage and set aside while you prepare dressing. Add Pineapple Dressing* and mix well. Refrigerate for one to two hours before serving. This salad is still delicious next day.

*PINEAPPLE SALAD DRESSING

1 cup MAYONNAISE
1 can (8½-oz.) CRUSHED PINEAPPLE
1 Tbsp. SUGAR
1 Tbsp. DRIED ONION (minced or chopped)
2 Tbsp. MILK
2 Tbsp. VINEGAR
1 tsp. CELERY SEED
½ tsp. GROUND MUSTARD

Combine all ingredients in a pint jar and mix well.

Pineapple-Citrus Salad

1 large GRAPEFRUIT
2 large ORANGES
1 can (8- to 9-oz.) PINEAPPLE CHUNKS (drained)
2 BANANAS
½ cup SALAD DRESSING
¼ cup APPLE SAUCE

Peel and section grapefruit and oranges (removing white membrane) and place in a salad bowl. Cut pineapple chunks in half and add to other fruit. Add sliced bananas. Mix salad dressing and apple sauce and mix into the fruits. (Serves 4)

Fresh Fruit & Pineapple Salad

1 can (16-oz.) PINEAPPLE CHUNKS (reserve juice)
2 APPLES (chopped)
2 BANANAS (sliced)
1 Tbsp. LEMON JUICE
1 cup whole GREEN GRAPES
2 ORANGES (sectioned and cut in half)

Drain pineapple and save juice for the dressing. (Apples may be peeled if you prefer.) Place first three ingredients in a bowl and sprinkle with lemon juice. Add rest of ingredients and toss to mix. Add enough Fresh Fruit Salad Dressing* to coat fruit and serve. (Serves 4 to 6)

*FRESH FRUIT SALAD DRESSING

1 cup SUGAR
2 Tbsp. FLOUR
1 cup LIQUID (pineapple juice from 16-oz. can pineapple, plus water to equal 1 cup of liquid)

In a small saucepan, combine sugar and flour. Slowly add liquid, stirring to mix. Heat over medium flame, stirring constantly while mixture thickens. Cool and use to coat fresh fruit. This dressing is good on any combination of fresh fruits.

Apple Nut Salad

2/3 cup MAYONNAISE
2 tsp. LEMON JUICE
2 red APPLES (unpeeled and chopped)
1 green APPLE (unpeeled and chopped)
1 cup CELERY (chopped)
½ cup WALNUTS (or peanuts, chopped)
¼ cup RAISINS

Mix mayonnaise and lemon juice. Place rest of ingredients in bowl and toss to mix. Add mayonnaise and stir to coat. (Serves 4 to 6)

Potato Salad

3 medium-size cooked POTATOES (diced)
4 EGGS (hard boiled)*
1½ cups SALAD DRESSING
½ cup MILK
2 Tbsp. VINEGAR
1 Tbsp. CELERY FLAKES
3 Tbsp. DRIED ONION (minced or chopped)
1 to 1½ tsp. GROUND MUSTARD (to taste)
2 Tbsp. PREPARED MUSTARD
½ tsp. PEPPER
½ tsp. SALT
PAPRIKA

Peel and dice cold potatoes and eggs into a bowl. Combine rest of ingredients (except paprika) and mix well. Stir into potato mixture and mix thoroughly. Sprinkle with paprika and chill well before serving. (Serves 4 to 6)

*Hint for Perfect Hard-Boiled Eggs: Place eggs in pan and cover with cold water. Add one tablespoon vinegar and bring to a rolling boil. Cover and remove from heat. Let sit for 15 minutes. Drain and run pan full of cold water. Peel when cool.

Olé Hamburger Salad

1 lb. HAMBURGER (lean)
1 pkg. (1¼-oz.) TACO SEASONING
¾ cup WATER
3 to 4 cups LETTUCE (shredded)
2 TOMATOES (finely-chopped)
1 cup CHEDDAR CHEESE (shredded)
1 cup CHUNKY SALSA (mild to hot)
TORTILLA CHIPS

Brown hamburger in a skillet and drain off all grease. Add taco seasoning and mix well. Stir in water and simmer for about 10 minutes, stirring occasionally as mixture thickens. Place lettuce in a large bowl and layer with hamburger, tomatoes, and cheese. Pour salsa over salad and serve with tortilla chips. (Serves 4)

This may be put together as four individual salads by placing one-fourth of ingredients in each bowl. Layer as above.

Italian Garden Salad

4 small plum or Italian TOMATOES (chopped)
2 small ZUCCHINI (sliced in chunks)
1 cup CAULIFLOWERETS
8 to 10 RADISHES (sliced thin)

Toss vegetables together and serve with an Italian style dressing.*
(Serves 4)

*ITALIAN DRESSING

¾ cup OLIVE OIL
¼ cup cider VINEGAR
2 Tbsp. SUGAR
1 Tbsp. DRIED PARSLEY
1 tsp. CELERY FLAKES
½ tsp. GROUND MUSTARD
½ tsp. ONION SALT
¼ to ½ tsp. GARLIC POWDER (to taste)

Combine all ingredients in a pint jar and shake to mix. Refrigerate
for two hours or more to allow flavors to blend. (1 cup)

Lemon Honey Salad Dressing

2/3 cup SUGAR
¼ cup white VINEGAR
1 cup SALAD OIL
½ cup HONEY
¼ cup LEMON JUICE
¼ tsp. GROUND MUSTARD
1 tsp. CELERY SEED

Combine ingredients in a jar and shake to mix. Good on fruit
salads. (Yield: about 2 cups)

Onion-Cucumber Salad in Yogurt

1 large CUCUMBER (or 2 small to medium)
1 medium size BERMUDA ONION
10 RADISHES (thinly-sliced)
1 container (8-oz.) plain YOGURT
¼ cup white VINEGAR
½ tsp. GROUND MUSTARD
2 tsp. SUGAR

Peel and slice cucumbers and onions in thin slices. Place cucumbers in a bowl. Separate onion slices into rings and place on top of cucumbers. Add sliced radishes. Combine remaining ingredients and mix into vegetables.

Citrus Salad

2 GRAPEFRUIT (peeled and sliced across sections)
2 ORANGES (peeled and sliced across sections)
2 KIWI FRUIT (peeled and sliced)

Divide fruit into four servings and arrange on a salad plate. Top with Italian Dressing or Lemon-Orange Salad Dressing*.

*LEMON-ORANGE SALAD DRESSING

¼ cup ORANGE JUICE
1 cup SALAD OIL
1 Tbsp. white VINEGAR
2 Tbsp. LEMON JUICE
1/3 cup SUGAR
1 Tbsp. DRIED ONION (minced or chopped)
1 tsp. CELERY SEED

Combine all ingredients in a pint jar and shake to mix. Refrigerate for one to two hours before using. (Yield: About 1½ cups)

Chicken Fruit Salad

3 cups cooked or canned CHICKEN (diced)
2 APPLES (unpeeled and diced)
1 can (16-oz.) PINEAPPLE CHUNKS (reserve juice)
1 cup MAYONNAISE
½ cup PINEAPPLE JUICE (add water
    if needed to equal ½ cup)
½ tsp. POPPY SEEDS (optional)

Combine first three ingredients in a bowl and mix. Combine rest of ingredients and mix well. Stir into the fruit. Chill prior to serving. (Serves 6 to 8)

Vegetable Salad

4 cups LETTUCE
1 can (16-oz.) diced MIXED VEGETABLES
3 Tbsp. BACON BITS
1 can (2.5-oz.) FRENCH-FRIED ONION RINGS

Combine lettuce and vegetables in a bowl and mix well. Sprinkle on bacon bits and onion rings. Serve with your favorite salad dressing. Our choice is Zesty Mexican Salad Dressing*.

*ZESTY MEXICAN SALAD DRESSING

1 cup MAYONNAISE
1 cup BUTTERMILK
1 to 2 Tbsp. CHILI POWDER (start with 1)
1 tsp. GROUND MUSTARD
1 Tbsp. DRIED PARSLEY
1 tsp. CELERY SEED
¼ tsp. OREGANO

Combine all ingredients and mix thoroughly. Refrigerate for one to two hours before using.

Stuffed Tomatoes

Cut off top of tomato one-quarter-inch from top. Scoop out insides. Stuff with one of the three recipes given here. Each recipe makes enough stuffing for four tomatoes.

DEVILED EGG & HAM STUFFING

1½ cups cooked or canned HAM (diced)
3 EGGS (hard-boiled and chopped)
½ cup SALAD DRESSING
3 Tbsp. MILK
1 Tbsp. PREPARED MUSTARD
1 tsp. DRIED PARSLEY

Combine ham and eggs in a bowl and mix. Stir rest of ingredients together and add to ham. Mix thoroughly. Serve in tomato cups.

SEAFOOD FILLING

1 can (6.5-oz.) CRAB MEAT (drained)
1 can (5-oz.) SMALL SHRIMP (drained)
1 can (6½-oz.) WATER CHESTNUTS (drained)
½ cup SALAD DRESSING
2 Tbsp. MILK
1 Tbsp. SOY SAUCE
¼ tsp. POWDERED GINGER

Flake crab into a bowl. (Check for shell bits and membrane.) Add shrimp and toss lightly to combine. Mince water chestnuts and add to seafood. Combine rest of ingredients and mix well. Fold into seafood. Serve in tomato cups.

TUNA FILLING

1 can (10-oz.) TUNA*
3 EGGS (hard-boiled and chopped)
½ cup CELERY (chopped)
½ cup SALAD DRESSING
1 Tbsp. MILK
½ tsp. GROUND MUSTARD
¼ tsp. DILL WEED (optional)

Flake tuna with juice into a bowl. Add eggs and celery. Combine rest of ingredients and add to tuna. Mix thoroughly. Serve in tomato cups.

*A can of boned chicken may be substituted for the tuna. Omit the dill weed.

Fresh Fish Salad

2½ to 3 cups cold FISH (flaked & boned)*
3 cups LETTUCE (shredded)
2 TOMATOES (cut each one into 4 wedges)

Flake and bone cold cooked fish and set aside. Divide lettuce into four servings and place on individual plates. Put one-quarter of fish on top each plate of lettuce. Add tomato wedges. Serve with Red Hot Salad Dressing** or Thousand Island Dressing***.

*This is a good way to use any leftover fish from the Barbecued Fish—Chinese Style in the Campfire Cooking section.
(Substitute two (5-oz.) cans of shrimp or two (6.5-oz.) cans of flaked crab for fish.)

**RED HOT SALAD DRESSING

1 cup CATSUP
1 Tbsp. LEMON JUICE
2 to 3 Tbsp. HORSERADISH (to taste)
½ tsp. GROUND MUSTARD

Mix all ingredients thoroughly.

***THOUSAND ISLAND DRESSING

1¼ cup MAYONNAISE
½ cup CATSUP
½ cup MILK
1 Tbsp. DRIED ONION (minced or chopped)
¼ cup SWEET PICKLE RELISH
1 tsp. GROUND MUSTARD

Combine all ingredients and mix thoroughly. Make two to three hours ahead and refrigerate to give flavors a chance to blend.

Simple Salad

4 wedges of LETTUCE
2 TOMATOES (sliced)
1 or 2 CARROTS (scraped and cut into sticks)

Make four servings by dividing ingredients and placing on four plates. Serve with Tomato Soup French Dressing*.

*TOMATO SOUP FRENCH DRESSING

1 can (10¾-oz.) CREAM OF TOMATO SOUP
1 cup cider VINEGAR
1½ cups SALAD OIL
1 cup SUGAR
3 Tbsp. WORCESTERSHIRE SAUCE
2 Tbsp. DRIED PARSLEY
1 Tbsp. CELERY FLAKES
1 tsp. GARLIC POWDER
1 tsp. GROUND MUSTARD

Combine ingredients in large jar and shake to mix. Refrigerate for two or more hours before serving. This is a good dressing to make before you leave home. Keeps well in the refrigerator and is delicious on any salad.

Macaroni & Tuna Salad

1 cup SALAD DRESSING
1/3 cup MILK
1 Tbsp. DRIED ONION (minced or chopped)
2 tsp. DRIED PARSLEY
1 tsp. CELERY FLAKES
½ tsp. GROUND MUSTARD
1 can (9¼-oz.) TUNA (flaked)
1 can (16-oz.) DICED MIXED VEGETABLES (drained)
2 cups cooked MACARONI SHELLS

Combine first six ingredients in a bowl and mix well. Set aside. Flake tuna into a salad bowl and add vegetables and cold macaroni. Add dressing mix and mix thoroughly. Chill before serving. (Serves 4)

Company Rice Salad

4 cups cold cooked INSTANT RICE
1½ cups cooked or canned HAM (or chicken), diced
1 can (16-oz.) PINEAPPLE CHUNKS (drained)
½ cup ALMONDS (sliced)
1/3 cup plain YOGURT
1/3 cup MAYONNAISE

   Mix all ingredients in order. Mix thoroughly and chill before serving. (Serves 4)

Seafood

Fresh or canned seafood is good for you and adds variety to your menu. Yes, that old stand-by "tuna" is in the book, but so is "Crab Casserole" and "Seafood Pie"!

Baked Fish with Tomato Sauce

4 lbs. FISH FILLETS
1 can (16-oz.) STEWED TOMATOES
1 can (4-oz.) mild DICED CHILIES (drained)
½ tsp. SWEET BASIL
2 Tbsp. DRIED ONION (minced or chopped)
1 Tbsp. DRIED PARSLEY
1 tsp. CELERY FLAKES
¼ tsp. GARLIC POWDER
¼ cup WHITE WINE (optional)

Place fish in shallow baking pan. Combine all of the ingredients except wine and pour over fish. Bake at 350 degrees for 45 minutes, or until fish flakes. Add wine, carefully spooning in to sauce. Return to oven for five to ten minutes and serve.

Fish Fillets Italiano

4 lbs. FISH FILLETS
1 bottle ITALIAN SALAD DRESSING

Marinate fish in dressing for two hours. Roll in coating* and fry in olive oil or cooking oil until fish flakes and is golden brown. For pan-size fillets, cooking time is about 15 minutes on each side.

*FISH COATING

1 cup CRACKER CRUMBS (finely crushed)
1 cup yellow CORNMEAL
¼ to ½ tsp. GARLIC POWDER (to taste)
1 tsp. CELERY SEED
1 Tbsp. PAPRIKA

Combine all ingredients and mix well. (2 cups)

Creamed Fish in White Sauce

¼ cup FLOUR
2¼ cups MILK (fresh or canned)
1 tsp. DRIED PARSLEY
¼ tsp. PEPPER
2 tsp. INSTANT CHICKEN BOUILLON
2 Tbsp. MARGARINE
2½ cups cooked FISH (boned and flaked)

Mix flour with about one cup of the milk in a saucepan. Mix until smooth. Slowly add rest of milk and stir until smooth. Add remaining ingredients except fish and cook over low heat, stirring constantly until mixture thickens. Add fish and mix well. Simmer for 10 minutes, or until fish is hot. If thinner sauce is preferred, thin by adding additional milk a spoonful at a time until you reach desired consistency. Serve over toast, biscuits or pasta. (Serves 2 or 3).

Cod Fillets in Crab Sauce

2 pkgs. (12-oz.) FROZEN COD

Defrost fish and dry. Place in a single layer in a baking pan. Cover with Crab Sauce* and bake at 375 degrees for 45 minutes. When tested with a fork, fish flakes when it is done. (Serves 4 or 5)

*CRAB SAUCE

¾ cup MILK (fresh or canned)
2 Tbsp. FLOUR
¼ tsp. GARLIC POWDER
¼ tsp. PEPPER
¼ tsp. DILL WEED (optional)
¼ cup WHITE WINE (or additional ¼ cup milk)
1 can (7½-oz.) CRAB MEAT
PAPRIKA

Pour milk into a saucepan, add flour and stir until smooth. Add rest of ingredients except crab and paprika. Heat milk, stirring constantly, until mixture starts to thicken. Remove from heat and flake crab into the sauce (checking for shell or membrane bits as you flake). Stir to mix and pour over cod. Sprinkle with paprika and bake per instructions.

Clam Fritters

2 cans (6.5-oz.) CHOPPED CLAMS (drain juice & reserve)
MILK (add enough milk to clam juice to make ½ cup liquid)
1 cup BUTTERMILK BAKING MIX
1 tsp. DRIED PARSLEY
1 Tbsp. DRIED ONION (minced or chopped)
1 EGG (beaten)
¼ tsp. SALT
COOKING OIL

Combine all ingredients except cooking oil and mix well. Heat ¼-inch of oil in fry pan and drop batter by spoonsful. Fry to golden brown on both sides. Drain on a paper towel and serve. (Serves 3 to 4)

Mock Lobster

1 pkg. (12-oz.) FROZEN COD
5 cups WATER
1 Tbsp. MARGARINE
1 tsp. SALT

Separate frozen cod fillets (or, if they are frozen in a solid block, use a serrated knife and cut into 4 pieces). Pour water into a large pan, add rest of ingredients and bring water to a rolling boil. Drop in frozen pieces of cod. Boil until fish turns white and rises to the top of the water. May be served hot with Lemon Butter* or cold with Hot Red Sauce.** (Serves 2 or 3)

*LEMON BUTTER

½ cup BUTTER (or margarine)
2 Tbsp. LEMON JUICE
1 to 2 drops TABASCO (optional)

Melt all ingredients together and serve hot.

**HOT RED SAUCE

1 cup CATSUP
2 Tbsp. LEMON JUICE
2 to 3 Tbsp. hot HORSERADISH (add to taste)

Combine all ingredients and mix well. Serve with cold fish, shrimp or crab. (makes 1 cup)

Easy Clam Chowder

1 can (19½-oz.) POTATO SOUP
1½ cups MILK
½ cup WATER
2 cans (6.5-oz.) chopped CLAMS
1 tsp. INSTANT CHICKEN BOUILLON
1 Tbsp. DRIED PARSLEY
1 Tbsp. DRIED ONION (minced or chopped)

Combine all ingredients and heat until hot. Stir occasionally. (Serves 4)

Crusty Crab Cakes

2 cans (6.5-oz.) CRAB MEAT (drained)
1 cup CRACKER CRUMBS (finely crushed)
2 Tbsp. WORCESTERSHIRE SAUCE
1 Tbsp. DRIED ONION (minced or chopped)
1 tsp. GROUND MUSTARD
½ tsp. CELERY SEED
¼ tsp. PEPPER
1 EGG (beaten)
3 to 4 Tbsp. MILK (just enough to hold it together)

Flake crab into a bowl. Remove shell bits. Add all ingredients and mix well. Shape into patties. Heat cooking oil and fry crab cakes until golden brown and crusty (about 10 minutes on each side). Serve with Zesty Mustard Sauce* or Hot Red Sauce. (Serves 4 to 6)

*ZESTY MUSTARD SAUCE

1½ Tbsp. FLOUR
1 cup WATER
1 tsp. INSTANT CHICKEN BOUILLON
½ to 1 Tbsp. HORSERADISH (to taste)
½ tsp. GROUND MUSTARD
2 tsp. PREPARED MUSTARD
1 Tbsp. MARGARINE

Mix flour with ¼-cup water in a saucepan and stir until smooth. Slowly add rest of water, stirring constantly to keep mixture smooth. Add rest of ingredients and mix well. Heat over low flame, stirring constantly as mixture thickens. Serve with crab dishes or salmon.

Oyster Stew

1 can (19½-oz.) POTATO SOUP
1 can (10¾-oz.) CREAM OF CELERY SOUP
2 cups MILK
¼ tsp. PEPPER
2 cans (10-oz.) OYSTERS (with liquid)
2 Tbsp. MARGARINE

Combine first four ingredients and mix well. Heat to boiling point. Add rest of ingredients and simmer for 10 minutes, stirring occasionally. (Serves 4 to 6)

Tuna-Macaroni Stove Top Casserole

1 pkg (8.7-oz.) MACARONI & CHEESE
1 can (9¼-oz.) TUNA (flaked)
1 can (4-oz.) DICED GREEN CHILIES (drained)
½ cup MILK

Prepare macaroni and cheese following directions on package. Add all ingredients to the hot macaroni and mix well. Cook over low heat in covered pan for about five minutes. Stir and serve. (Serves 4 to 6)

Tuna & Rice Hot Dish

1½ cups uncooked INSTANT RICE
1 can (9¼-oz.) TUNA (flaked)
1 tsp. CELERY FLAKES
1 Tbsp. DRIED ONION (minced or chopped)
1 EGG (beaten)
1½ cups MILK (fresh or canned)
½ cup CHEDDAR CHEESE (shredded)
PAPRIKA

Combine first seven ingredients in a bowl and mix well. Pour into a greased casserole and sprinkle with paprika. Bake at 350 degrees for 45 minutes to one hour or until rice is tender. (Serves 4)

Salmon Loaf

2 cans (16-oz.) SALMON (drain & reserve liquid)
MILK (add milk to salmon juice to make 1½ cups liquid)
1 Tbsp. DRIED ONION (minced or chopped)
1 Tbsp. CELERY FLAKES
¼ tsp. DILL WEED (optional)
2 EGGS (beaten)
3 cups coarse CRACKER CRUMBS
2 tsp. GROUND MUSTARD
½ tsp. PEPPER

Flake salmon into bowl, removing any skin and bones. Add rest of ingredients and mix thoroughly. Spoon into a greased loaf pan. Bake at 350 degrees for 45 minutes to one hour. (Serves 6 to 8)

Seafood Chowder Supreme

1 can (16-oz.) CREAMED CORN
1 can (16-oz.) STEWED TOMATOES
1 can (19½-oz.) POTATO SOUP
4½ cups WATER
3 Tbsp. INSTANT CHICKEN BOUILLON
2 Tbsp. DRIED PARSLEY
3 Tbsp. DRIED ONION (minced or chopped)
2 Tbsp. CELERY FLAKES
1 tsp. SWEEET BASIL
1 tsp. GARLIC POWDER
½ tsp. PEPPER
½ tsp. DILL WEED
2 cans (6.5-oz.) CRAB MEAT (drained and flaked)
2 cans (5-oz.) SHRIMP (drained)
2 cans (6½-oz.) CHOPPED CLAMS
1 can (8-10 oz.) small OYSTERS
1 can (9¼-oz.) TUNA (flaked)
½ cup WHITE WINE (or additional ½ cup water)

Combine first 12 ingredients in a large pot. Bring to a boil and simmer for 10 to 15 minutes. (Check crab for shell bits as you flake it.) Add rest of ingredients except wine. Simmer for 20 minutes, stirring occasionally. Add wine, heat an additional 10 minutes and serve. (Serves 8 to 10)

This is a good chowder for a crowd because you may stretch it by adding up to two additional cups of water and three teaspoons of instant chicken bouillon.

Shrimp Jambalaya

½ lb. LINK SAUSAGE
1 can (16-oz.) STEWED TOMATOES
1 cup WATER
2 Tbsp. DRIED ONION (minced or chopped)
2 tsp. INSTANT CHICKEN BOUILLON
1½ tsp. CHILI POWDER
¼ tsp. THYME
1 can (4-oz.) DICED CHILIES (drained)
2 cans (5-oz.) SMALL SHRIMP* (drained)
1 cup INSTANT RICE (uncooked)

Slice sausages into small pieces and fry in a large skillet until done. Drain off grease. Add tomatoes and break up any large pieces with a fork. Add the rest of the ingredients, in order, up to the shrimp. Stir to mix and simmer for 15 minutes. Add shrimp and continue to simmer for five more minutes. Add rice, stir to mix. Cover and remove from heat and let sit for five minutes. (Serves 4)

*Fresh shrimp may be used. Shell and clean about 18 medium-size shrimp. Cut into bite-size. Add at the same point canned shrimp is added but simmer until shrimp turn pink (about five to 10 minutes). Do not overcook. Add rice and complete recipe as stated above.

Salmon Patties

1 Tbsp. DRIED ONION (minced or chopped)
1 tsp. CELERY FLAKES
1 tsp. GROUND MUSTARD
¼ tsp. PEPPER
½ cup MILK (fresh or canned)
1 can (16-oz.) SALMON
1 EGG (beaten)
1½ cups CRACKER CRUMBS (finely chopped)
3 Tbsp. COOKING OIL (add more if needed)

Combine the first five items and set aside. Flake salmon into a bowl, removing any skin and bones. Add milk mixture and rest of ingredients. Shape into patties. Heat oil in a skillet and fry patties until brown and crispy on the outside. Add oil if needed. Serve with Zesty Mustard Sauce or lemon wedges. (Serves 4 to 6)

Seafood Pie

2 cans (6.5-oz.) CRAB MEAT (drained)
1 can (7½-oz.) TUNA
2 cans (5-oz.) SMALL SHRIMP (drained)
1 cup CHEDDAR CHEESE (shredded)
1¼ cups MILK
¾ cup BUTTERMILK BAKING MIX
3 EGGS (beaten)
1 can (4-oz.) DICED CHILIES (drained)
1 tsp. CELERY FLAKES
PAPRIKA

Grease a 10-inch pie pan (or use an 8 x 8 pan) and flake crab, removing any shell bits, into the pan. Add tuna and shrimp. Distribute evenly. Sprinkle with ½ of the cheese. Combine the milk, baking mix, eggs, chilies and celery flakes and mix well. Pour over the seafood. Sprinkle with rest of cheese and paprika. Bake at 400 degrees for 35 minutes or until knife inserted in middle comes out clean.

Fifteen-Minute Salsa Shrimp

1 can (8-oz.) TOMATO SAUCE
½ cup CHUNKY SALSA
1 cup WATER
2 cans (5-oz.) SMALL SHRIMP*
1½ cups INSTANT RICE (uncooked)

Combine first four ingredients in a saucepan and stir to mix. Simmer for 10 minutes. Stir in rice, cover and remove from heat. Let sit for five minutes, stir and serve. (Serves 4)

*Fresh shrimp may be used. Shell and clean about 18 medium-size shrimp. Cut into bite size pieces and simmer in sauce until they turn pink. This may not take the full 10 minutes. Do not overcook. Add rice, remove from heat, cover and let sit for five minutes before serving. (Serves 4)

Shrimp Rice Cakes

½ cup INSTANT RICE
½ cup WATER
1 tsp. INSTANT CHICKEN BOUILLON
2 cans (5-oz.) SMALL SHRIMP (drained)
1 EGG (beaten)
¾ cup CRACKER CRUMBS (finely crushed)
½ tsp. GROUND MUSTARD
2 to 3 Tbsp. MILK (enough to hold cakes together)
2 to 3 Tbsp. COOKING OIL

Combine rice, water and bouillon in a small pan and bring to a boil. Cover and remove from heat. Set aside to cool. Mash shrimp and add all of the ingredients except the oil. Mix well. Add cold rice and mix thoroughly. Shape into flat cakes. Heat two tablespoons oil in a skillet and fry cakes about 10 minutes on each side (until golden brown). Add oil if needed. Serve alone or with Hot Red Sauce. (Serves 4)

Crab Casserole

2 cans (6.5-oz.) CRAB MEAT (drained)
1 cup stale BREAD CRUMBS
2 EGGS (beaten)
1 cup MILK (fresh or canned)
½ cup MAYONNAISE
1 tsp. CELERY FLAKES
1 tsp. INSTANT CHICKEN BOUILLON
PAPRiKA

Flake crab into a bowl and remove any shell bits. Add rest of ingredients except paprika and mix well. Place in a greased casserole, sprinkle with paprika and bake at 350 degrees for 45 minutes to one hour. (Serves 4)

Fresh Meat Recipes

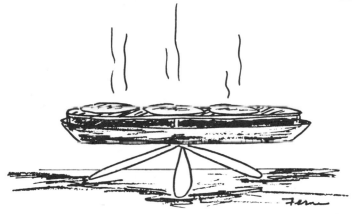

Many campers spend a few days at several locations during their trips. If you are traveling in this manner, stop at a store on "travel day" and pick up some fresh meat. We have included several recipes that are easy to prepare and take little cooking time.

Smothered Meat Loaf

1 lb. lean GROUND BEEF
½ tsp. GROUND SAGE
½ tsp. SALT
1 tsp. CELERY FLAKES
½ cup SODA CRACKER CRUMBS (finely-crushed)
1 Tbsp. WORCESTERSHIRE SAUCE
1 pkg (8-oz.) PORK LINK SAUSAGE
1 can (10¾-oz.) FRENCH ONION SOUP

Combine the first six ingredients in a bowl and mx well. Slice sausages into four slices each and add to the ground beef. Mix well. Shape into a loaf and put in a loaf pan. Bake at 350 degrees for one-half hour. Drain off any grease; cover with onion soup and return to oven and bake an additional 30 minutes. Let sit five minutes before slicing. (Serves 4)

Variation: Instead of sage, add ½ tsp. oregano. Instead of onion soup, cover with one cup of mild to hot chunky salsa.

*Rainy Day Roast

1 (5-lb.) ROAST (round bone, 2-3 inches thick)
½ tsp. PEPPER
2 Tbsp. VINEGAR
2 Tbsp. WORCESTERSHIRE SAUCE
2 Tbsp. COOKING OIL

Sprinkle roast on both sides with pepper. Rub each side with a tablespoon of vinegar and Worcestershire sauce. Pierce all over with a fork and refrigerate for one hour. Heat oil in a fry pan (if pan is Teflon, heat without oil) and brown roast on both sides. Cover with Simmer Sauce** and roast on top of the stove, covered until tender (about 2 to 3 hours). Add water as needed. Add potatoes and vegetables one hour before roast is done, if you want to cook a one-pot meal. Roast this size will serve four with enough left over for Machaca Beef.

**SIMMER SAUCE

1 cup WATER
1 tsp. INSTANT BEEF BOUILLON
3 Tbsp. DRIED ONION (minced or chopped)

Combine all ingredients and pour over Rainy Day Roast.

*Called Rainy Day Roast because it takes so long, we only cook it on a rainy day when we can't be outdoors anyway.

Hamburger Chile Hot Dish

1 lb. LEAN HAMBURGER
3 Tbsp. DRIED ONION (minced or chopped)
1½ to 2 Tbsp. CHILI POWDER
1 Tbsp. CELERY FLAKES
1 can (8-oz.) TOMATO SAUCE
1 can (16-oz.) STEWED TOMATOES
1 can (15-oz.) RED KIDNEY BEANS
2 cups uncooked INSTANT RICE

In skillet, brown hamburger and drain off all grease. Add next six ingredients and mix well. Simmer for 20 minutes, stirring occasionally. Add rice and mix in well. Cover; remove from heat and let sit for five minutes. Stir and serve. (Serves 6)

Simmered Steak

2 to 3 lbs. ROUND STEAK
¼ cup FLOUR
1 tsp. SEASONED SALT
½ tsp. PEPPER
2 Tbsp. OLIVE OIL (or cooking oil)
½ to 1 cup WATER

Cut steak into serving-size pieces. Combine flour, salt and pepper. Pound flour mixture into both sides of the steak. Use the edge of an unbreakable plate or cup. Heat oil in a fry pan and brown steak on both sides. Add one-half cup of water, cover and simmer for 30 to 45 minutes until tender. Add water as needed. Cover with Celery Sauce * (or Tomato Sauce**) and cook an additional 15 to 20 minutes.

*CELERY SAUCE

1 can (10¾-oz.) CREAM of CELERY SOUP
¾ soup can WATER
1 Tbsp. DRIED ONION (minced or chopped)

Combine all ingredients and mix well. Pour over steak.

**TOMATO SAUCE

1 can (16 oz.) STEWED TOMATOES
1 can (4 oz.) DICED CHILIES (drained)
1 Tbsp. DRIED ONION (minced or chopped)
2 CARROTS (scraped & sliced thin) (optional)

Combine all ingredients and pour over steak.

Machaca Beef

2 cups ROAST BEEF (shredded)
1 cup CHUNKY SALSA (mild to hot)

Heat beef and salsa together. May be served alone or with small flour tortillas to wrap the beef in.

Salsa Hamburger Steak

1 lb. of lean HAMBURGER
1 Tbsp. DRIED ONION (minced or chopped)
1 Tbsp. WORCESTERSHIRE SAUCE
1 tsp. INSTANT BEEF BOUILLON
½ tsp. CELERY SEED
1½ cups SALSA (medium to hot)
1 can (2.5-oz.) FRENCH FRIED ONION RINGS

Combine first five ingredients and mix well. Shape into four hamburger steaks, about one-half-inch thick. Heat fry pan (if not Teflon coated add two tablespoons oil) and brown hamburger on both sides. Drain off any grease, cover meat with salsa and simmer until done the way you like it. Serve with spoonful of sauce and sprinkle of onion rings. (Serves 4)

Rice Meatballs

1 lb. HAMBURGER (lean)
½ cup INSTANT RICE (uncooked)
1 Tbsp. DRIED ONION (minced or chopped)
1 Tbsp. CHILI POWDER
½ tsp. SEASONED SALT
½ tsp. CELERY SEED
¼ tsp. GARLIC POWDER
3 Tbsp. CATSUP
1 Tbsp. WORCESTERSHIRE SAUCE
1 can (16-oz.) STEWED TOMATOES
1 Tbsp. INSTANT BEEF BOUILLON
½ cup WATER
1 Tbsp. CORNSTARCH

Combine first nine ingredients in a bowl and mix well. Shape into about 12 meatballs and place in a baking pan. Combine tomatoes with rest of the ingredients and pour over meatballs. Cover with foil and bake at 375 degrees for 30 minutes. Remove foil and bake for an additional 30 minutes. (Makes about 12 meatballs)

Stove Top Baked Hamburger

1 lb. lean HAMBURGER
½ tsp. ONION SALT
1 can (10¾-oz.) CREAM of MUSHROOM SOUP
½ soup can of WATER
2 tsp. INSTANT BEEF BOUILLON
1 tsp. CELERY FLAKES
1 can (4-oz.) SLICED MUSHROOMS

Press raw hamburger into the bottom of a skillet. Sprinkle with onion salt. Fry over medium heat until cooked part way through (about 10 minutes). Using a spatula, break hamburger into four servings. Turn over and continue cooking while you make the sauce. Combine the rest of the ingredients. Drain off grease from fry pan. Loosen hamburger and pour on sauce. Simmer for 15 to 20 minutes or until sauce is well blended and bubbly. Good served with rice, mashed potatoes or noodles. (Serves 4)

Sweet & Sour Meatballs

1 lb. LEAN HAMBURGER
2 Tbsp. DRIED ONION (minced or chopped)
½ tsp. GARLIC POWDER
¾ cup SODA CRACKER CRUMBS (finely-crushed)
1 Tbsp. SOY SAUCE
1 EGG (beaten)
¼ cup CATSUP

Combine all ingredients and mix well. Make small meatballs and place in a baking pan. Cover with Spicy Cranberry Sauce* and bake at 350 degrees for 45 minutes. Baste occasionally. (Serves 4 to 6)

*SPICY CRANBERRY SAUCE

1 cup WHOLE CRANBERRY SAUCE
1 cup CHILI SAUCE
¼ cup BROWN SUGAR (packed)
2 Tbsp. VINEGAR

In saucepan, combine all ingredients. Simmer until cranberry sauce melts and ingredients are blended. Pour over meatballs.

Enchilada Hot Dish

1 lb. HAMBURGER (lean)
1 Tbsp. DRIED ONION (minced or chopped)
1 can (16-oz.) TOMATOES
1 can (8-oz.) TOMATO SAUCE
1 Tbsp. CHILI POWDER
1 tsp. CELERY FLAKES
1 tsp. INSTANT BEEF BOUILLON
1 bag (15½-oz.) CORN CHIPS (crushed)
1 cup CHEDDAR CHEESE (shredded)

   Brown hamburger in hot skillet. Drain off grease. Add onion and mix. Cut tomatoes into small pieces and add with tomato sauce, chili powder, celery flakes and bouillon to hamburger. Mix well. Simmer five minutes. Place one-half of meat mixture in a baking pan; cover with one-half of chips and cheese. Repeat layer, ending with cheese. Bake at 350 degrees for 35 minutes. (Serves 4 to 6)

Mexican Pizza

1 lb. HAMBURGER (lean)
3 Tbsp. TACO SEASONING
2 FLOUR TORTILLAS (large)
1 can (16-oz.) REFRIED BEANS
1 cup CHUNKY SALSA (mild to hot)
1 cup MOZZARELLA CHEESE (or cheddar, shredded)
2 cups LETTUCE (shredded)
2 TOMATOES (chopped fine)
½ cup RIPE OLIVES (pitted)

   Heat skillet and brown hamburger. Drain off all grease. Add taco seasoning and mix well. Cook over low heat for five minutes stirring constantly. Place tortillas on a cookie sheet that is covered with foil. Spread each tortilla with one-half can of beans, top with one-half of hamburger, one-half of salsa and one-half of cheese. Preheat oven to 375 degrees and bake pizzas until cheese is melted and bubbly (about 15 minutes). Top each pizza with one-half of the lettuce, tomatoes and olives. Serve with additional salsa on the side, if desired.

Mexican Hamburger Pie

1 lb. HAMBURGER (lean)
¼ tsp. SWEET BASIL
¼ tsp. OREGANO
1 Tbsp. CHILI POWDER
1 tsp. CELERY FLAKES
¾ cup CHUNKY SALSA (mild to hot)
½ cup BUTTERMILK BAKING MIX
1 cup MILK (fresh or canned)
2 EGGS (beaten)
1 Tbsp. DRIED ONION (minced or chopped)
2 slices (¾-oz. each) PROCESSED CHEESE
PAPRIKA

Brown beef in a skillet and drain off grease. Add next four ingredients and mix well. Place meat in bottom of a greased nine-inch pie pan. Spoon salsa evenly over meat. Combine baking mix with milk, eggs and onion and mix thoroughly. Pour over meat. Cut cheese into strips and lay across the pie; sprinkle with paprika and bake at 375 degrees for 45 minutes or until knife inserted in the middle of the pie comes out clean. (Serves 4)

Tortilla Beef Bake

1 lb. HAMBURGER (lean)
2 Tbsp. DRIED ONION (minced or chopped)
1½ to 2 Tbsp. CHILI POWDER (to taste)
¼ tsp. GARLIC POWDER
1 tsp. CELERY SEED
1 tsp. INSTANT BEEF BOUILLON
1 can (16-oz.) STEWED TOMATOES
1 can (8-oz.) TOMATO SAUCE
1 can (4-oz.) DICED CHILIES
6 FLOUR TORTILLAS (medium size)
2 cups CHEDDAR CHEESE (shredded)
1½ cups SOUR CREAM

Brown beef in a skillet and drain off all grease. Add the next eight ingredients and mix well. Simmer for 10 minutes. Place one-third of the hamburger mixture in a baking pan; cover with three tortillas, overlapping as necessary. Sprinkle with one-third of the cheese. Repeat layers ending with cheese. Bake at 375 degrees for 45 minutes. Serve with sour cream. (Serves 4 to 6)

Chileburgers

1 lb. HAMBURGER (lean)
1½ tsp. CHILI POWDER
1 can (16-oz.) CHILI CON CARNE (with beans)
½ cup WATER
4 HAMBURGER BUNS
1 cup CHEDDAR CHEESE (shredded)
1 can (2.5-oz.) FRENCH-FRIED ONION RINGS

Combine hamburger with chili powder and mix well. Shape into four patties. Fry in hot skillet until done the way you like. (May be grilled over the campfire.) Combine chili con carne with water and heat until hot and bubbly. Toast buns (if desired) and place halves side by side on individual plates. Place hamburger on bun halves and cover each with one-quarter chili, cheese and onion rings.

Meatball Soup

1 lb. HAMBURGER (lean)
1 tsp. CELERY FLAKES
1 Tbsp. DRIED ONION (minced or chopped)
2 cups WATER
4 cups TOMATO JUICE
1½ Tbsp. INSTANT CHICKEN BOUILLON
1 can (16-oz.) CREAMED CORN
½ tsp. OREGANO
½ tsp. GROUND CUMIN
½ tsp. GARLIC POWDER
½ cup INSTANT RICE

Mix hamburger with celery flakes and onion and shape into bite-size meatballs. Brown the meatballs in a large saucepan. Drain off any grease and add rest of the ingredients in the order given. Stir carefully to blend without breaking up the meatballs. Simmer uncovered for 30 minutes. Serve hot. (Serves 6)

Sloppy Scrambled Hamburgers

1½ to 2 lbs. HAMBURGER (lean)
1 can (10¾-oz.) CREAM of TOMATO SOUP
½ soup can WATER
2 Tbsp. WORCESTERSHIRE SAUCE
3 Tbsp. DRIED ONION (minced or chopped)
1½ Tbsp. CELERY FLAKES
2 to 3 Tbsp. CHILI POWDER (to taste)
1 Tbsp. INSTANT BEEF BOUILLON
1 can BEER
2 cups CHEDDAR CHEESE (shredded)*
HAMBURGER BUNS

Lightly brown hamburger and drain off grease. Add next seven ingredients and mix well. Simmer for 20 minutes, stirring occasionally. Add beer and stir to blend. Simmer 10 minutes. Serve over split buns with a sprinkle of cheese. (Serves 8 to 10)

*If you are out of cheese, spread buns with the soft cheese spread that comes in a jar, spoon on the hamburger and serve.

This is an easy recipe to prepare for a camping "pot luck." You may simmer it for much longer than the time given and it can be cooked over a campfire. If it cooks down too much, just add soup, water or beer.

Beef Short Ribs
in Chunky Tomato Sauce

2 to 3 meaty SHORT RIBS per person
(or use stew meat)

Place meat in a pan and barely cover with water. Simmer until tender. Watch water level, as this can boil dry if fire is too high. When tender, drain water, add Chunky Tomato Sauce* and simmer for about one hour, turning meat occasionally.

*CHUNKY TOMATO SAUCE

1 can (16-oz.) TOMATOES (cut tomatoes up)
½ cup VINEGAR
2 Tbsp. WORCESTERSHIRE SAUCE
2 Tbsp. DRIED ONION (minced or chopped)
¼ cup BROWN SUGAR (packed)
½ to 1 tsp. GARLIC POWDER (to taste)
1 Tbsp. CELERY FLAKES
1 tsp. GROUND MUSTARD

Combine all ingredients in a pan and simmer for 10 minutes. Stir to mix well and pour over beef ribs or stew meat.

Hamburger-Cornbread Upside Down Cake

1 lb. HAMBURGER (lean)
1½ Tbsp. CHILI POWDER
1 can (4-oz.) DICED GREEN CHILIES (drained)
1 can (8-oz.) STEWED TOMATOES
1 can (12-oz.) CORN NIBLETS (drained)
1 small pkg. CORNBREAD MIX (size for 8 x 8 pan)
½ cup CHEDDAR CHEESE (shredded)

Brown hamburger and drain off grease. Add chili powder, chilies and tomatoes and mix well. Spoon into 9 x 9 baking pan. Spread corn over hamburger. Make cornbread following directions on package, adding one-fourth cup cheese. Pour over hamburger. Sprinkle with cheese and bake for 35 minutes (or until the cornbread is done). May be cut into squares and served or turned out as an upside down cake. Lay a large sheet of foil over the pan, fold the edges down around the pan and place a platter on top of the foil. Turn over, cut and serve. (Serves 4 to 6)

Chinese Hamburger Over Chow Mein Noodles

1 lb. HAMBURGER (lean)
2 Tbsp. SOY SAUCE
1 Tbsp. CELERY FLAKES
1 Tbsp. INSTANT BEEF BOUILLON
1 can (10¾-oz.) CREAM of MUSHROOM SOUP
3½ cups WATER (reserve ½ cup)
1 can (16-oz.) CHOW MEIN VEGETABLES (drained)
2½ Tbsp. CORNSTARCH
CHOW MEIN NOODLES

Brown hamburger in a large pan and drain off grease. Add ingredients except one-half cup water and cornstarch. Mix and put aside. Stir hamburger mixture to blend and simmer for 15 minutes. Bring to boiling point and add water and cornstarch mixture, stirring constantly as the mixture thickens. Serve over chow mein noodles. (Serves 3 to 4)

Stuffed Baked Hamburger

2 lbs. HAMBURGER (lean)
1½ cups WATER
1 can (10¾-oz.) CREAM of CHICKEN SOUP
1 can (10¾-oz.) CREAM of CELERY SOUP
2 Tbsp. DRIED ONION (minced or chopped)
1 Tbsp. DRIED PARSLEY
4½ cups BREAD STUFFING CUBES (seasoned)
PAPRIKA

Press raw beef into the bottom of a greased 9 x 13 baking pan. In a saucepan, combine water, soups, onion and parsley. Mix well and simmer for 10 minutes. Add stuffing cubes and toss to coat. Spread mixture over raw hamburger and sprinkle with paprika. Bake at 350 degrees for one hour. Cut in squares to serve. (Serves 6 to 8)

Hamburger & Cabbage In Tomato Sauce

1 lb. HAMBURGER (lean)
1½ cups INSTANT RICE (uncooked)
1 small CABBAGE (shredded)
1 can (10¾-oz.) CREAM of TOMATO SOUP
1 soup can WATER
½ tsp. OREGANO
1 tsp. INSTANT BEEF BOUILLON

Lightly brown hamburger and drain grease. Mix with the rice. Spoon into a greased baking pan. Place cabbage on top of meat. Mix remaining ingredients until well blended and pour over cabbage. Cover with foil and bake at 350 degrees for 45 minutes (or until cabbage is tender). Tastes similar to stuffed cabbage. (Serves 4 to 6)

Beef & Mushroom Hot Dish

1 lb. HAMBURGER (lean)
2 Tbsp. DRIED ONION (minced or chopped)
1 can (4-oz.) MUSHROOMS BITS & PIECES (drained)
1 can (10¾-oz.) CREAM of MUSHROOM SOUP
¾ cup WATER
1 tsp. INSTANT BEEF BOUILLON
1½ cups INSTANT RICE (uncooked)

Brown beef and drain off grease. Add next five ingredients and mix well. Bring to a boil, add rice and mix. Cover pan and remove from heat. Let sit five minutes. Stir and serve. (Serves 4 to 6)

Easy Sausage Pizzas

1 lb. BULK SAUSAGE
2 Tbsp. TACO SEASONING
2 Tbsp. WATER
1 can (8-oz.) TOMATO SAUCE
1 cup CHEDDAR CHEESE (shredded)
8 ENGLISH MUFFINS (toasted)

Brown sausage and drain off grease. Add seasoning, water and tomato sauce and mix well. Mix in cheese. Remove from heat and spread on toasted muffin halves. Put under broiler until cheese melts and is browned and bubbly.

Best Barbecued Pork Back Ribs

      3 to 4 lbs. lean PORK BACK RIBS
      4 cups WATER
      2 Tbsp. PICKLING SPICE
      1 Tbsp. BROWN SUGAR

   Place ribs in large pan and add all ingredients. Water should barely cover ribs. Bring to slow boil and cook 1½ hours or until tender. (Allow 2 to 3 ribs per person.) Place ribs in single layer in a shallow baking pan and add Easy Barbecue Sauce*. Bake ribs 30 to 40 minutes in 350 degree oven. Turn and baste 2 or 3 times during baking time.

*EASY BARBECUE SAUCE

      1 cup hot BARBECUE SAUCE
      ½ cup light CORN SYRUP
      2 Tbsp. DRIED ONION (minced or chopped)
      ½ to 1 tsp. GROUND MUSTARD (adds zip)

Combine all ingredients and use for pork, beef or chicken.

Pork Soup

      2 cups PORK (cooked and diced)
      1 can (15-oz.) PINTO BEANS
         (or 2 cups cooked pinto beans)
      1 can (14½-oz.) WHITE HOMINY
      5 cups WATER
      5 Tbsp. INSTANT CHICKEN BOUILLON
      1 to 2 Tbsp. GARLIC POWDER (to taste)
      4 Tbsp. DRIED ONION (minced or chopped)
      CHUNKY SALSA
      FRESH CHIVES (chopped) (optional)

   Combine first seven ingredients in a pan and simmer for 30 minutes. Stir occasionally. Serve in bowls with a spoonful of salsa and a sprinkle of chives. (Serves 4)

Saucy Barbecued Chicken Wings

16 CHICKEN WINGS

Singe wings if needed and clip wing tip and discard. Divide wing at the half joint. Place in a shallow roasting pan in a single layer and bake at 350 degrees for 30 minutes. Turn once during baking time. Add Brown Sugar Barbecue Sauce* and bake 30 minutes (or until tender). Baste and turn wings during final cooking time. (Serves 4)

*BROWN SUGAR BARBECUE SAUCE

    1 cup BARBECUE SAUCE
    ¼ cup BROWN SUGAR
    ¼ cup WATER
    1 Tbsp. DRIED ONION (minced or chopped)
    2 Tbsp. SOY SAUCE
    ½ tsp. POWDERED GINGER
    1 tsp. GROUND MUSTARD
    1 tsp. CORNSTARCH

Combine all ingredients in a small saucepan and simmer for five minutes, stirring constantly. Use on chicken wings.

Baked Chicken

4 lbs. CHICKEN (breasts and thighs)
4 POTATOES (scrubbed & peeled, if you prefer)
1 can (10¾-oz.) CREAM of MUSHROOM SOUP
¾ soup can WATER
1 Tbsp. CORNSTARCH (mixed with the water)
1 Tbsp. SOY SAUCE
1 tsp. INSTANT CHICKEN BOUILLON
1 tsp. CELERY FLAKES
1 can (4-oz.) MUSHROOM BITS & PIECES (drained)
½ tsp. PEPPER
1 can (2.5-oz.) FRENCH-FRIED ONION RINGS
PAPRIKA

Using serving size pieces of chicken, skin chicken and place in a single layer in a greased baking dish. Slice potatoes and place on top of the chicken. Combine rest of ingredients except onion rings and paprika. Mix well and pour over the potatoes. Sprinkle onion rings and paprika over the sauce and bake at 350 degrees for one hour or until chicken and potatoes are tender. (Serves 4 to 6)

Chili Chicken

4 CHICKEN BREASTS (split)
1 tsp. SEASONED SALT
1 to 2 Tbsp. OLIVE OIL (or cooking oil)
1 can (16-oz.) STEWED TOMATOES
1 tsp. INSTANT CHICKEN BOUILLON
1 Tbsp. DRIED ONION (minced or chopped)
1½ Tbsp. CHILI POWDER
1 Tbsp. SUGAR
1 tsp. CELERY FLAKES
1 tsp. GARLIC POWDER
¼ cup WATER
1 can (2.5-oz.) FRENCH-FRIED ONION RINGS

Sprinkle skinned chicken with seasoned salt. Heat oil and brown chicken. In a bowl, combine rest of ingredients except the onion rings. Mix well and add to the chicken. Heat to boiling point, turn down heat and simmer for 45 minutes (or until chicken is tender). Serve covered with sauce and a sprinkle of onion rings. (Serves 4).

Rice is nice with this dish. Use instant rice and follow instructions on package, adding one teaspoon instant chicken bouillon for each cup of water.

Chicken & Rice

2 or 3 CHICKEN BREASTS (skin & pound flat)
1 Tbsp. MARGARINE
1½ cups WATER
1 Tbsp. INSTANT CHICKEN BOUILLON
1 Tbsp. DRIED ONION (minced or chopped)
1 Tbsp. DRIED PARSLEY
1 tsp. CELERY SEED
1 can (6½-oz.) WATER CHESTNUTS (sliced)
1½ cups INSTANT RICE (uncooked)
SOY SAUCE

After you have pounded chicken flat, cut into strips. Melt margarine and saute chicken until done (about 15 minutes). Add water, bouillon, onion, parsley, celery seed and water chestnuts. Bring to slow boil and cook for 10 minutes. Add rice and mix well. Cover and remove from heat. Let sit five minutes and serve with soy sauce or Sweet Sauce*. (Serves 4)

*SWEET SAUCE

1 cup GRAPE JELLY (melted)
1 tsp. CHILI POWDER
½ cup CHILI SAUCE

Heat all ingredients in a small pan. Sauce is ready when jelly is melted and ingredients are hot and well blended.

Recipe Notes

_____

_____

_____

_____

_____

_____

_____

_____

_____

_____

_____

_____

_____

_____

_____

_____

_____

_____

_____

_____

_____

_____

_____

Main Dish Meals
Using Canned Meats

Canned meats contain enough salt to satisfy most taste buds. In many instances, we use a variety of spices in our recipes but do not use additional salt.

We suggest you try the recipe the way it is listed. If you find you need additional salt, make a notation on the recipe.

We have also found that the instant bouillons add flavor as well as salt to food. For convenience, we prefer the instant crystals. They are available in regular or low sodium content. We use them as a salt replacement throughout the book.

Quick Skillet Stew

2½ cups WATER (reserve ½ cup)
1 can (16-oz.) STEWED TOMATOES
1 Tbsp. DRIED ONION (minced or chopped)
1 Tbsp. DRIED PARSLEY
1 Tbsp. INSTANT BEEF BOUILLON
1 can (12-oz.) ROAST BEEF & GRAVY
3 Tbsp. CORNSTARCH
1 can (16-oz.) whole POTATOES (drained)
1 can (16 oz.) whole small CARROTS (drained)

In a large skillet, combine two cups water with next four ingredients. Cut beef into small pieces and add it and the gravy. Mix well. Bring to a boil. Mix remaining water with cornstarch and add to beef, stirring costantly as mixture thickens. Add potatoes and carrots. Spoon gravy over vegetables. Cover pan and simmer for 15 minutes. (Serves 3 to 4)

Easy Beef Stroganoff

1 box (6-oz.) EGG NOODLES
3½ cups WATER (reserve ½ cup to mix with cornstarch)
2 Tbsp. INSTANT BEEF BOUILLON
1 tsp. CELERY FLAKES
1 Tbsp. DRIED ONION (minced or chopped)
1 Tbsp. DRIED PARSLEY
1 can (4-oz.) MUSHROOMS (drained)
1 can (12-oz.) ROAST BEEF & GRAVY
3 Tbsp. CORNSTARCH
½ cup SOUR CREAM
¼ cup WHITE WINE

Cook noodles following directions on the box. In a saucepan, combine three cups of water with bouillon, celery flakes, onion, parsley and mushrooms. Shred beef with a fork and add it and the gravy to the water. Simmer for 10 minutes. Mix rest of water with cornstarch and add to beef mixture. Stir constantly as mixture thickens. Add sour cream and wine, heat through and serve over noodles. (Serves 3 to 4)

Roast Beef Hash

1 pkg (6-oz.) HASH BROWN POTATOES
1 can (12-oz.) ROAST BEEF & GRAVY
½ cup WATER
1 tsp. CELERY SEED
1 Tbsp. DRIED PARSLEY
2 Tbsp. DRIED ONION (minced or chopped)

Cook potatoes according to directions on package Brown lightly. Shred beef chunks with a fork and add beef and gravy to potatoes. Mix well. Combine remaining ingredients and let set for 5 to 10 minutes. Mix all ingredients thoroughly and continue to cook over a medium flame. Turn hash occasionally with spatula. Hash is ready when it is hot and crusty. This may be baked in a greased casserole at 350 degrees for 30 minutes. (Serves 4)

Chinese Beef

1 can (12-oz.) ROAST BEEF & GRAVY
1 can (6½ oz.) sliced WATER CHESTNUTS
1 can (4 oz.) sliced MUSHROOMS
2 Tbsp. SOY SAUCE
3½ cups WATER (reserve ½ cup)
2 tsps. CELERY SEED
1 Tbsp. INSTANT BEEF BOUILLON
3 Tbsp. CORNSTARCH
CHOW MEIN NOODLES

Shred beef into saucepan. Add rest of ingredients except one-half cup water and cornstarch and chow mein noodles. Bring beef mixture to a boil; turn down and simmer for 10 minutes. Mix one-half cup water and cornstarch and add to beef. Stir constantly as mixture thickens. Serve over chow mein noodles. (Serves 3 to 4)

Chili Beef & Red Beans

1 can (12-oz.) ROAST BEEF & GRAVY
1 can (16-oz.) RED BEANS (or kidney beans)
1 can (16 oz.) STEWED TOMATOES WITH ONIONS
3½ cups WATER
1 Tbsp. CELERY FLAKES
1 Tbsp. DRIED ONION (minced or chopped)
1 Tbsp. INSTANT BEEF BOUILLON
1 tsp. SWEET BASIL
1½ Tbsp. CHILI POWDER
½ cup CATSUP

Shred beef and combine all ingredients in a saucepan. Bring to a boil, lower heat and simmer for 15 minutes. Serve in bowls with hot bread or crackers. (Serves 3 to 4)

Pepper Beef

1 can (12-oz.) ROAST BEEF & GRAVY
1 can (4-oz.) DICED CHILIES (drained)
3 cups WATER (reserve ½ cup)
1 Tbsp. DRIED ONION (minced or chopped)
¼ tsp. GARLIC POWDER
2 Tbsp. INSTANT BEEF BOUILLON
3 Tbsp. CORNSTARCH
INSTANT RICE

Shred beef into a pan and combine with gravy, chilies, 2½ cups of water, onion, garlic powder and bouillon. Mix well and heat to boiling point; turn down and simmer for five minutes. Mix one-half cup of water with the cornstarch and add to beef mixture, stirring constantly as mixture thickens. Serve over rice. Use directions on rice package for appropriate number of servings. (3 to 4 servings)

Almost Instant
Hot Beef Sandwich

1 can (12-oz.) ROAST BEEF & GRAVY
3 cups WATER (reserve ½ cup)
3 Tbsp. CATSUP
2 Tbsp. INSTANT BEEF BOUILLON
2 tsp. DRIED ONION (minced or chopped)
2 Tbsp. CORNSTARCH
INSTANT MASHED POTATOES
BREAD

Break beef chunks apart and combine them with gravy, 2½ cups of water, catsup, bouillon and onion. Mix well and heat over medium flame for 15 minutes. Mix one-half cup of water with cornstarch and add to beef. Stir constantly as mixture thickens. Prepare instant mashed potatoes according to directions on the package. Make sandwiches with the hot beef, cut in half and place a serving of mashed potatoes between the sandwich halves. Cover with gravy. (Serves 2 or 3)

Beef Macaroni Hot Dish

1 pkg. (6 to 8-oz. uncooked) MACARONI
1 can (12-oz .) ROAST BEEF & GRAVY
1 can (10 to 11-oz.) MUSHROOM SOUP
1 can (4-oz.) MUSHROOM BITS & PIECES (drained)
½ cup WATER
2 drops TABASCO (optional)
4 slices (¾-oz. each) CHEESE SLICES

Cook macaroni following directions on the package. Shred beef and add it and rest of ingredients (except cheese) to cooked macaroni. Pour into greased baking pan; cover with cheese slices and bake at 350 degrees for 30 to 35 minutes or until cheese is melted and hot dish is browned on top. (Serves 4)

Beef Biscuit Pie

2 cans (12-oz.) ROAST BEEF & GRAVY
1 can (16-oz.) whole POTATOES
1 can (16-oz.) STEWED TOMATOES WITH ONION
1 tsp. GARLIC POWDER
1 Tbsp. CELERY FLAKES
2 tsp. INSTANT BEEF BOUILLON
BUTTERMILK BAKING MIX

Cut beef chunks into small pieces and spread them in the bottom of an 8-inch square baking pan. Cut potatoes in half and place on top of beef. Combine stewed tomatoes with the rest of the ingredients down to the buttermilk baking mix. Pour mixture over beef and potatoes.
Using recipe on the box of mix, prepare the rolled biscuit dough. Pat or roll dough into an 8x8 square and place it over the meat mixture. Bake at 400 degrees for 25 minutes or until biscuits are brown. If biscuits appear to be browning too fast, cover loosely with foil for part of the cooking time. It takes 15 to 20 minutes for the meat and potatoes to heat through. (Serves 4 or 5)

Hearty Chile Hot Dish

2 cans (16-oz.) CHILE CON CARNE WITH BEANS
1 can (8-oz.) TOMATO SAUCE
1 Tbsp. DRIED ONION (minced or chopped)
1 tsp. CELERY SEED
1 Tbsp. CHILI POWDER
1¼ cups INSTANT RICE

Combine all ingredients except rice in a saucepan and heat to a boil. Add rice and mix well. Cover and remove from heat. Let stand for 5 minutes. More or less rice may be used for juicier or drier hot dish. (Serves 4 to 6)

Chile Corn Pie

1 can (16-oz.) CHILE CON CARNE WITH BEANS
1 can (12-oz.) ROAST BEEF & GRAVY
1 can (12-oz.) CORN NIBLETS
1 can (8-oz.) TOMATO SAUCE
1 can (4-oz.) DICED CHILIES (drained)
1 Tbsp. DRIED ONION (minced or chopped)
1 tsp. INSTANT BEEF BOUILLON
1 cup CHEDDAR CHEESE (shredded)
1 pkg. (6-oz.) CORN CHIPS (crushed)

In a bowl, combine first seven ingredients. Mix well and layer one-half meat, one-half cheese and one-half chips in a baking pan. Add second layer in same order. Bake at 350 degrees for 30 to 35 minutes. (Serves 4 to 6)

Chile Pie

1 can (16-oz.) CHILE CON CARNE WITH BEANS
2 Tbsp. DRIED ONION (minced or chopped)
1 cup CHEDDAR CHEESE (shredded)
½ cup BUTTERMILK BAKING MIX
1 cup MILK (fresh or canned)
2 EGGS (slightly beaten)
PAPRIKA

Spread chile in an 8- or 9-inch pie pan and sprinkle with onion and one-half cup cheese. Combine baking mix, milk and egg and mix well. Pour over chile; sprinkle with rest of cheese and paprika. Bake at 400 degrees for about 35 minutes. Knife should come out clean when inserted into middle of the pie. (Serves 3 or 4)

Shredded Beef Mexi Roll-Ups

1 can (12-oz.) ROAST BEEF & GRAVY
1 Tbsp. CHILI POWDER
1 Tbsp. DRIED ONION (minced or chopped)
½ cup SLICED RIPE OLIVES
1 cup CHEDDAR CHEESE (shredded)
2 cups ENCHILADA SAUCE
8 CORN TORTILLAS

Shred beef with a fork and combine with first three ingredients. Mix thoroughly. Add one-half cup cheese. Heat enchilada sauce in saucepan and dip each tortilla in sauce. Fill with one-eighth of meat mixture, roll and place seam side down in a lightly greased baking pan. Pour enchilada sauce over tortillas and sprinkle with rest of cheese. Bake at 350 degrees for about 30 minutes or until sauce is bubbly and cheese is melted. Serve with shredded lettuce and refried beans. (Serves 4)

Corn Beef Hash

1 cup MILK (fresh or canned)
2 Tbsp. DRIED ONION (minced or chopped)
1 Tbsp. DRIED PARSLEY
1 tsp. CELERY SEED
1 Tbsp. FLOUR
3 cups COOKED POTATOES (diced)
2 Tbsp. MARGARINE
1 can (12-oz.) CORN BEEF

Combine first five ingredients and set aside. Melt margarine in a skillet and brown potatoes. Cut up corn beef, add to potatoes and mix thoroughly. Stir in milk mixture and mix well. Cover and cook over low heat for 20 minutes, stirring occasionally. May be baked in a greased casserole at 350 degrees for 35 minutes. (Serves 4 to 6)

Creamed Corn Beef &
Peas on Toast

1 can (12-oz.) CORN BEEF
1 can (10¾-oz.) CELERY SOUP
1 soup can WATER
1 can (16-oz.) SMALL PEAS & PEARL ONIONS (drained)

Shred corn beef and combine all ingredients in a pan. Heat over medium heat for 10 to 15 minutes, stirring occasionally. When hot, serve over toast. (Serves 4 to 6)

Irish Stew

1 small head CABBAGE
4 small sweet WHITE ONIONS
1 tsp. CELERY FLAKES
1 tsp. INSTANT CHICKEN BOUILLON
WATER
1 can (16-oz.) POTATOES (drained)
1 can (12-oz.) CORN BEEF*

Cut cabbage in half, slice into thin wedges and place in a large pan. Peel onions and put on top of cabbage. Sprinkle in the celery flakes and bouillon. Add enough water to just cover the vegetables. Cover pan and simmer 15 to 20 minutes. Add potatoes. Slice corn beef and place on top of potatoes. Cover and continue to simmer until cabbage is tender (about 15 minutes). (Serves 3 or 4)

*Refrigerate corn beef overnight and it will slice easily.

Turkey with Orange Glaze

1 TURKEY ROAST

Bake turkey roast according to directions. Twenty minutes before end of cooking time, pour Orange Glaze* over turkey. Baste occasionally during final cooking time.

*ORANGE GLAZE

1 jar (10-oz.) ORANGE MARMALADE
¼ tsp. powdered GINGER
2 Tbsp. LEMON JUICE
1 Tbsp. WATER

Combine all ingredients in a small saucepan. Stir constantly as marmalade melts and ingredients blend. When marmalade is completely melted, glaze is ready to use.

Oriental Turkey

2 cups cooked TURKEY (diced)
1 can (10¾-oz.) CREAM of CHICKEN SOUP
1 soup can WATER
1 can (6.5-oz.) SLICED WATER CHESTNUTS (drained)
2 Tbsp. SOY SAUCE
2 cups CHOW MEIN NOODLES

Combine first five ingredients in a saucepan. Mix well and heat to boiling point. Turn heat down and simmer for 10 minutes, stirring occasionally. Add noodles, mix thoroughly and serve. (Serves 3 or 4)

Chicken Patties

1 can (10½-oz.) BONED CHICKEN
1 cup SODA CRACKER CRUMBS (finely crushed)
¼ cup MILK (fresh or canned)
1 EGG (slightly beaten)
1 tsp. CELERY SEED
1 Tbsp. SOY SAUCE
¼ cup SESAME SEEDS (optional)
2 to 3 Tbsp. COOKING OIL

Combine first six ingredients and mix well. Form into eight balls and roll balls in sesame seeds. Heat oil in fry pan; flatten chicken into patties and fry until golden brown on both sides (about 10 minutes on each side). Add oil if needed.

Chicken Goody Hot Dish

1½ cups canned or cooked CHICKEN
1 can (10¾-oz.) CREAM of CHICKEN SOUP
¼ cup WATER
¼ cup MAYONNAISE
1 Tbsp. SOY SAUCE
1 Tbsp. DRIED ONION (minced or chopped)
1 Tbsp. DRIED PARSLEY
1¼ cups uncooked INSTANT RICE
½ cup CHEDDAR CHEESE (shredded)
PAPRIKA

Combine first eight ingredients and mix well. Pour into greased casserole. Sprinkle with cheese and paprika. Bake at 350 degrees for one hour. (Serves 4 to 6)

Sweet & Sour Chicken

1 can (16-oz.) CRUSHED PINEAPPLE
½ cup BROWN SUGAR (packed)
½ cup VINEGAR
½ cup CATSUP
½ tsp. powdered GINGER
1 tsp. CELERY SEED
1 can (4-oz.) MILD CHILIES (drained)
1½ cups WATER (reserve ½ cup)
1 can (10-oz.) BONED CHICKEN
2 Tbsp. CORNSTARCH

In a saucepan, combine first seven ingredients. Add one cup water and mix well. Cut chicken into small pieces and add to pineapple mixture. Heat to boiling point; turn down heat and simmer for 10 minutes. Mix cornstarch with one-half cup water and add to chicken, stirring constantly while mixture thickens. Serve over instant rice. (Serves 3 to 4)

Chinese Chicken & Rice

1½ cups WATER
1 can (10¾-oz.) CREAM of CHICKEN SOUP
1 can (6.5-oz.) SLICED WATER CHESTNUTS
1 Tbsp. DRIED ONION (minced or chopped)
1 Tbsp. DRIED PARSLEY
1 tsp. CELERY FLAKES
1 can (10-oz.) BONED CHICKEN
1½ cups uncooked INSTANT RICE
¼ cup SLIVERED ALMONDS (optional)
SOY SAUCE

Combine first six ingredients in a saucepan. Flake chicken into mixture and mix well. Heat to boiling point; turn down heat and simmer for 15 minutes. Add rice and mix well. Cover and remove from heat. Let stand five minutes before serving. Serve with a sprinkle of almonds and soy sauce. (Serves 4)

Chicken Mexicana

1 can (8-oz.) REFRIED BEANS
1½ cups CHUNKY SALSA (mild to hot)
1 can (10-oz.) BONED CHICKEN (shredded)
2 cups TORTILLA CHIPS (crushed)
1 EGG (beaten)
½ cup MILK (fresh or canned)
1¼ cup CHEDDAR CHEESE (shredded)

Combine beans and salsa in a bowl and mix well. Add chicken and rest of ingredients (except one-quarter cup cheese). Mix thoroughly and pour into a greased casserole. Sprinkle with the one-quarter cup cheese and bake at 350 degrees for 45 minutes to an hour.

Easy Chicken Burro

1 can (10-oz.) BONED CHICKEN (shredded)
1 can (4-oz.) DICED CHILIES (drained)
8 small FLOUR TORTILLAS
8 Tbsp. soft processed CHEESE SPREAD (in a jar)

Combine chicken and chilies in a saucepan and heat until hot. Warm tortillas and spread each one with one tablespoon of cheese spread. Put one-eighth of chicken and chili mix down the center of each tortilla. Fold up ends of tortilla to help hold mixture in and roll from the opposite side. Serve seam side down on a plate. May be served with a topping of sour cream, salsa or Avocado Topping*. Shredded lettuce is a nice addition if desired.

*AVOCADO TOPPING

3 AVOCADOS (peeled and mashed)
½ cup CHUNKY SALSA

Combine avocado and salsa and mix thoroughly.

Easy Creamed Chicken

1 can (10-oz.) BONED CHICKEN
1 can (10¾-oz.) CREAM of CHICKEN SOUP
¾ soup can WATER
1 can (4-oz.) MUSHROOMS BITS & PIECES (drained)
2 Tbsp. SOY SAUCE
2 tsp. CORNSTARCH
¼ cup WHITE WINE (or milk)

Flake chicken into a saucepan and combine with next four ingredients. Mix well and heat to boiling point; turn down heat and simmer for 10 minutes, stirring occasionally. Mix cornstarch with wine and add to chicken, stirring constantly as mixture thickens slightly. Serve on toast or mashed potatoes. (Serves 3-4)

Chicken & Dumplings

2 cans (10-oz.) BONED CHICKEN
2 cans (10¾-oz.) CREAM of CHICKEN SOUP
2 soup cans WATER
1 Tbsp. DRIED PARSLEY

Cut chicken into small pieces and combine with rest of ingredients in a saucepan. Heat to boiling point; turn down heat and simmer for 10 minutes, stirring occasionally. Add dumplings and cook as directed on the dumpling recipe.* (Serves 4 to 6)

*DUMPLINGS

2 cups BUTTERMILK BAKING MIX
2/3 cup MILK (fresh or canned)
1 tsp. CELERY SEED

Combine all ingredients and mix well. Drop by spoonsful on top of boiling chicken mixture. Cook 10 minutes uncovered and 10 minutes covered. Spoon chicken over dumplings to serve. (Makes 10 to 12 dumplings.)

Easy Chicken Stew*

1 can (10¾-oz.) CREAM of CHICKEN SOUP
1 can (10¾-oz.) CREAM of CELERY SOUP
2 soup cans WATER
2 cans (10-oz.) BONED CHICKEN
1 can (16-oz.) POTATOES (drained)
1 can (16-oz.) small WHOLE CARROTS (drained)
1 can (8 to 10-oz.) GREEN PEAS (drained)

In a skillet or large saucepan, combine soups and water and mix well. Cook to simmer. Break chicken into pieces and add to soup. Simmer for 10 minutes. Add vegetables and heat about 10 minutes or until vegetables are hot.

*This recipe may be baked in the oven. Blend soups and water in a baking dish and add rest of the ingredients in order. Using buttermilk baking mix, make biscuit recipe on the box. Bake stew at 350 degrees for 25 minutes and turn oven to 400 degrees; place biscuits on top of stew and bake until biscuits are done.

Baked Chicken & Dressing

2 cans (10-oz.) BONED CHICKEN
1 can (4-oz.) SLICED MUSHROOMS
2 cups INSTANT STUFFING MIX
1¼ cups HOT WATER
2 Tbsp. MARGARINE

Cut chicken into pieces and spread in the bottom of a greased 8 x 8 baking pan. Spread mushrooms and juice over chicken. Mix stuffing mix with hot water and spoon over chicken. Dot with margarine and cover with a sheet of aluminum foil. Bake at 350 degrees for 25 minutes; remove foil and bake about 10 minutes or until top is brown. (Serves 4 to 6)

Ham-Yam Bake

1 canned (1-lb.) HAM
1 can (16-oz.) YAMS (dry packed)
1 can (16-oz.) CRUSHED PINEAPPLE
½ cup BROWN SUGAR (packed)
1 Tbsp. DRIED ONION (minced or chopped)
1 tsp. GROUND MUSTARD
½ tsp. GROUND CLOVES

Place ham in an 8 x 8 baking pan. Put yams around the ham. Combine rest of ingredients and pour over ham and yams. Bake at 350 degrees for 45 minutes to an hour. (Serves 4)

Ham-Bean Bake

1 can (16-oz.) CUT GREEN BEANS (drained)
1 can (16-oz.) RED BEANS (or kidney beans, drained)
1 can (16-oz.) LIMA BEANS (drained)
1 canned (1-lb.) HAM
1¼ cups mild to hot BARBECUE SAUCE
¼ cup CORN SYRUP

Combine beans in a greased baking pan. Cut ham into bite-size pieces and place on top of beans. Mix barbecue sauce and syrup and pour over beans and ham. Stir to mix. Bake at 350 degrees for about one hour, stirring occasionally. (Serves 4 to 6)

Scalloped Ham & Potatoes

1 canned (1-lb.) HAM
1 pkg (5.25 to 6-oz.) AU GRATIN POTATOES
1 Tbsp. DRIED PARSLEY
1 Tbsp. DRIED ONION (minced or chopped)
½ cup CHEDDAR CHEESE (shredded)

Cut ham into bite-size pieces. Mix potatoes in a casserole, following directions on the package. Add ham, parsley and onion. Stir to mix. Sprinkle on cheese and bake at 350 degrees for one hour or until potatoes are tender and top is browned. (Serves 4 to 6)

Stove Top Baked Ham

1 canned (1-lb.) HAM
2 Tbsp. MARGARINE

Brown ham in margarine in a pan that has a cover. Cover with Cranberry Ham Sauce* and cook, covered, over low heat for 30 to 45 minutes. Baste often.

*CRANBERRY HAM SAUCE

1 cup WHOLE CRANBERRY SAUCE
¼ tsp. GROUND CLOVES
1 tsp. GROUND MUSTARD
¼ cup BROWN SUGAR (packed)

Melt cranberry sauce in a small saucepan. Add rest of the ingredients. Stir and heat until ingredients are thoroughly blended.

Variation: This sauce is good on chicken if you omit the cloves and add one-quarter teaspoon ginger.

Ham & Cheese with Noodles

1 pkg. (6 to 8-oz.) EGG NOODLES (or spinach noodles)
1 canned (1-lb.) HAM (diced)
2 cans (11-oz.) CHEESE SOUP
1½ soup cans MILK (fresh or canned)
1 Tbsp. WORCESTERSHIRE SAUCE
1½ tsp. GROUND MUSTARD
1 tsp. CELERY SEED

Cook noodles according to directions on package. Combine rest of ingredients in a saucepan and mix well. Heat to boiling point; turn heat down and simmer uncovered for 15 minutes. Stir occasionally. Serve over hot noodles. (Serves 4 to 6)

Cheesy Ham & Rice

1 canned (1-lb.) HAM (diced)
1 can (11-oz.) CHEESE SOUP (plus WATER to
    make 2¼ cups of liquid)
1 can (4-oz.) DICED CHILIES (drained)
2 cups uncooked INSTANT RICE

Combine ham, soup, water and chilies in a saucepan. Heat to a rolling boil. Add rice and mix well. Cover pan, remove from heat and let stand for five minutes. Stir and serve. (Serves 4 to 6)

Hot Ham Sandwich

1 canned (1-lb.) HAM (diced or cut in strips)
1 can (10¾-oz.) CREAM of TOMATO SOUP
½ cup MILK (fresh or canned)
1 can (4-oz.) DICED CHILIES (drained)
1 cup CHEDDAR CHEESE (shredded)

Combine all ingredients in a saucepan and mix well. Heat over medium heat until cheese is melted and ham is hot. Serve on toast or buns. (Serves 4 to 6)

Grilled Deviled Ham & Cheese Sandwich

8 slices BREAD
2 cans (2¼-oz.) DEVILED HAM
4 Tbsp. SOFT CHEESE SPREAD (comes in a jar)
MARGARINE

For each sandwich: spread one slice of bread with one-half can of deviled ham and the other slice with a tablespoon of cheese spread. Do not spread the cheese all the way to the edges. Put sandwich together and lightly butter the top slice. Heat fry pan and place sandwich in pan, buttered side down. Butter the other slice. Fry until brown, turn over and fry other side until brown. Serve sandwiches hot.

Macaroni & Cheese Supreme

1 pkg. (7 or 8-oz.) MACARONI & CHEESE
1 can (10¾-oz.) CREAM OF MUSHROOM SOUP
1 can (4-oz.) MUSHROOMS BITS & PIECES (drained)
½ cup MILK (canned or fresh)
¼ cup BACON BITS (optional)
1 cup CHEDDAR CHEESE (shredded)

Cook macaroni according to instructions on the package. Drain and place in greased casserole. Sprinkle with cheese that comes in the macaroni package. Combine soup, mushrooms, milk, bacon bits and one-half cup of the cheese. Pour over macaroni and stir to mix. Sprinkle with rest of cheese and bake at 350 degrees for about 45 minutes or until it is bubbly and top is browned.

Variations: Instead of mushroom soup, mushrooms and bacon bits, use cream of celery soup, one can (4-oz.) diced chilies (drained) and one cup diced, cooked or canned ham.

For a chicken dish, replace bacon bits with a can (5 to 7-oz.) of chicken. Flake chicken and mix it into dish.

Vegetables

In some areas, local farmers bring their produce to the camp-grounds. We take advantage of door to door selling and replenish our fresh vegetable supply.

Company Green Beans

1 can (15- to 16-oz.) CUT GREEN BEANS
3 Tbsp. BACON BITS
½ cup canned FRENCH-FRIED ONION RINGS

Combine beans and bacon bits and heat for 10 minutes or until beans are hot. Drain and either toss with onion rings or serve with onion rings sprinkled on top. (Serves 3 to 4)

Gingered Carrots

¼ cup MARGARINE
3 Tbsp. BROWN SUGAR
¼ tsp. POWDERED GINGER
1 can (16- to 18-oz.) SMALL WHOLE CARROTS (drained)
1 can (8-oz.) ORANGE SLICES (drained)

Melt margarine and stir in brown sugar and ginger. Stir until sugar is dissolved. Add carrots and oranges and spoon sauce over them to coat. Simmer for 10 minutes, stirring often as carrots heat. Serve when hot. (Serves 3 to 4)

Tomato & Green Bean Bake

1 can (16-oz.) TOMATOES
1 can (16-oz.) WHOLE GREEN BEANS (drained)
1 can (4-oz.) DICED CHILIES (drained)
¼ cup MILK
¼ cup BACON BITS
1 can (2.5-oz.) FRENCH-FRIED ONION RINGS

Break up tomatoes with a fork and combine with all ingredients except onion rings. Place in baking pan and sprinkle with onion rings. Bake at 350 degrees 20 to 30 minutes or until bubbly. (Serves 6)

Red, White & Green Bean Relish

1 can (16-oz.) CUT GREEN BEANS (drained)
1 can (15-oz.) RED KIDNEY BEANS (drained)
1 can (15½-oz.) GARBANZO BEANS (drained)
2/3 cup VINEGAR
½ cup SUGAR
3 Tbsp. DRIED ONION (minced or chopped)
1 Tbsp. CORNSTARCH
½ tsp. CELERY SEED

Combine beans in a container that has a cover. Mix all the rest of the ingredients in a small saucepan and heat, stirring constantly as mixture thickens. Simmer three to five minutes. Pour hot mixture over the beans and mix well. Refrigerate until well chilled. Keeps well several days in the refrigerator.

Barbecued Beans

1 can (16-oz.) FRENCH-STYLE GREEN BEANS
1 can (15-oz.) WHITE GREAT NORTHERN BEANS
1 can (15-oz.) LIMA BEANS
1 cup BARBECUE SAUCE
¼ cup light CORN SYRUP
1 Tbsp. DRIED ONION (minced or chopped)
1 tsp. CELERY FLAKES

Oven Method: Drain beans and place in a shallow baking pan. Combine rest of ingredients and mix well. Pour over beans. Bake at 350 degrees for 20 to 30 minutes until bubbly. Stir occasionally. (Serves 6 to 8)

Stove Top Method: Drain beans and combine in a large pot. Combine the rest of the ingredients and add to beans. Mix well. Cover and simmer for about 20 minutes, stirring occasionally.

Sweet & Sour Beans

½ cup WATER
½ cup VINEGAR
½ cup BROWN SUGAR (packed)
4 Tbsp. DRIED ONION (minced or chopped)
1 Tbsp. GROUND MUSTARD
2 Tbsp. FLOUR
2 cans (16-oz.) PORK AND BEANS

Stove-Top Method: Combine water and vinegar in a large pan. Mix sugar, onion, mustard and flour together. Add to water. Mix in well. Cook over low heat, stirring constantly while mixture thickens. Add beans at once and stir in quickly. Cook over low flame until beans are hot (about 15 minutes). (Serves 4 to 6)

Oven Method: Combine all ingredients and mix thoroughly. Bake in greased casserole for 45 minutes at 350 degrees. Stir occasionally.

Pickled Beets Relish

1/3 cup VINEGAR
¼ cup SUGAR
2 tsp. PICKLING SPICE
1 cup BEET JUICE (add water to make 1 cup)
1 Tbsp. CORNSTARCH
1 can (16-oz.) SLICED BEETS

Combine all ingredients except beets in a saucepan. Heat over medium flame, stirring constantly until mixture thickens. Add beets and simmer for 15 minutes. Stir occasionally. May be served hot or cold.

Corn & Tomato Stove-Top Casserole

1 can (15-oz.) CREAM-STYLE CORN
1 can (16-oz.) STEWED TOMATOES
1 can (4-oz.) DICED CHILIES
¼ tsp. GARLIC POWDER
1 cup SEASONED SALAD CROUTONS

Combine first four ingredients in a saucepan and simmer for 15 minutes. When mixture is hot, stir in croutons and mix well. Serve at once in bowls. (Serves 4 to 6)

Zucchini-Tomato Bake

3 cups raw ZUCCHINI (sliced)
1 can (16-oz.) STEWED TOMATOES
1½ cups SEASONED SALAD CROUTONS
1 can (2.5-oz.) FRENCH-FRIED ONION RINGS
½ cup CHEDDAR CHEESE (shredded)

Place sliced zucchini in a shallow baking pan. Spread tomatoes over zucchini. Sprinkle croutons and onion rings evenly over the vegetables. Bake at 350 degrees for 25 minutes. Sprinkle on cheese and return to oven for 10 minutes or until cheese is melted and lightly browned. (Serves 4)

Potato Cakes

1 pkg. (6-oz.) HASH BROWN POTATOES
¼ cup MILK
½ cup FLOUR
1 EGG (beaten)
1 tsp. CELERY SEED
¼ tsp. PEPPER
2 to 3 Tbsp. COOKING OIL

Place potatoes in a pan and cover with four cups water. Bring to a boil; turn off and let stand uncovered for 15 minutes. Drain and let cool. Combine all of the remaining ingredients with cold potatoes. Mix thoroughly and make into patties. Heat two tablespoons of oil in a skillet and fry patties until golden brown on both sides. Add oil as needed. (Serves 4)

Indian Corn Bake

2 EGGS (slightly beaten)
1 can (16-oz.) CREAM-STYLE CORN
1 can (12-oz.) CORN NIBLETS
1 cup coarse SODA CRACKER CRUMBS (reserve ¼ cup)
2 Tbsp. DRIED ONION (minced or chopped)
1 Tbsp. DRIED PARSLEY
½ tsp. PEPPER
½ tsp. SALT
½ cup MILK (fresh or canned)
2 Tbsp. MARGARINE
PAPRIKA

Beat eggs, add corn and three-fourths cup crumbs. Add rest of ingredients in order down to the margarine. Mix thoroughly and pour into a greased casserole. Sprinkle with rest of crumbs, dot with margarine and sprinkle with paprika. Bake at 375 degrees for one hour. (Serves 6)

Marinated Carrots & Artichokes

1 jar (6½-oz.) ARTICHOKE HEARTS IN JUICE
1 can (16-oz.) small WHOLE CARROTS (drained)
1 jar (2-oz.) diced PIMENTO (drained)
2 cans (4-oz.) whole MUSHROOMS (drained)
2/3 cup white VINEGAR
1 tsp. CELERY SEED
1 tsp. POWDERED GARLIC
1 tsp. SWEET BASIL
2 tsp. SUGAR
1 Tbsp. DRIED ONION (minced or chopped)

Cut up artichoke hearts, combine with juice and next three ingredients. In a saucepan, mix vinegar with rest of ingredients and heat to boiling point. Lower heat and simmer for five minutes. Pour hot marinade over the vegetables. Cover and refrigerate over night. Next day, drain off marinade and discard. Serve chilled vegetables. (Serves 3 to 4)

Corn Fritters

2 EGGS (beaten)
½ cup MILK (fresh or canned)
2 tsp. DRIED ONION (minced or chopped)
1 tsp. CELERY FLAKES
¼ tsp. PEPPER
1¼ cups BUTTERMILK BAKING MIX
1 can (16-oz.) CORN NIBLETS
3 to 4 Tbsp. COOKING OIL

Combine all ingredients in order given and mix thoroughly. Heat three tablespoons oil in skillet and drop batter by the spoonful into hot oil. Brown well (about eight minutes on each side). Add oil as needed. Serve hot plain or with maple syrup. (Serves 4)

Easy Desserts

Desserts that are easy to prepare are a must for the traveling cook. Many of our recipes use foods that have a long shelf life. You can have desserts at the end of the trip, as well as the beginning.

Fruit Whip

2 EGG WHITES (beaten stiff)
1/3 cup SUGAR
2 cans (small) JUNIOR BABY FRUIT (any fruit)
1 cup non-dairy WHIPPED TOPPING

Beat egg whites until stiff and fold in sugar as you beat. Fold in rest of ingredients in order. Chill and serve.

Chocolate Velvet Dessert

1 pkg. (4-serving size) INSTANT CHOCOLATE PUDDING
1 cup MILK
1½ cups non-dairy WHIPPED TOPPING

Place pudding mix in a bowl and add milk. Beat until well mixed and thick. Fold in whipped topping and chill before serving.

Fresh Fruit Slush

3 large ORANGES
3 BANANAS
2 LEMONS
¾ cup SUGAR
1 cup WATER

Peel and section oranges and cut into small pieces. Mash bananas and add to oranges. Squeeze and grate lemons into the fruit mixture. Combine sugar and water in a small pan and bring to a boil. Boil five minutes. Cool and mix with the fruit. Freeze mixture in an ice tray. Stir occasionally as fruit freezes. Mixture will stay slushy.

Easy Frozen Fruit Cream

1 cup fresh PEACHES (sliced)*
¼ cup SUGAR
1 tsp. LEMON JUICE
20 MARSHMALLOWS
¼ cup WATER
1 cup WHIPPING CREAM

In a bowl, crush fruit with sugar and mix well. Add lemon juice. Melt marshmallows in water, stirring constantly. Add to fruit mixture and mix well. Let it cool. Whip cream very stiff and fold into cold fruit mixture. Freeze in freezer tray for several hours until firm. Slice to serve.

*Fresh strawberries or raspberries may be used instead of peaches.

Double Chocolate Nut Dessert

½ cup GRAHAM CRACKER CRUMBS (or vanilla wafer)
1 pkg. (4-serving size) INSTANT CHOCOLATE PUDDING
1½ cups MILK (fresh or canned)
1 cup non-dairy WHIPPED TOPPING
¼ cup CHOCOLATE ICE CREAM TOPPING
½ cup WALNUTS (chopped)

Place crumbs in an ice tray. Make pudding using 1½ cups milk. Fold in whipped topping. Spoon pudding into ice tray. Drizzle chocolate topping over pudding and sprinkle with nuts. Freeze until solid enough to slice (about three to four hours). If it freezes too solid, leave out of freezer for 10 to 15 minutes before serving.

Black Cherry Vanilla Dessert Cups

1 pkg. (4-serving size) BLACK CHERRY JELL-O
1 pkg. (4-serving size) INSTANT VANILLA PUDDING

Prepare Jell-O following directions on package and refrigerate until soft set. Prepare pudding following directions on package. Using individual dessert cups, layer Jell-O and pudding in cups*. Start with Jell-O and end with pudding. May be topped with whipped topping. Refrigerate for two hours or until Jell-O is completely set before serving. Make up only what you will use, as this dessert does not keep well over night.

*The six to eight ounce clear plastic glasses make nice dessert cups for the traveler. They are lightweight "throw-aways" but may be washed and reused many times.

Pineapple Balls

½ cup CRUSHED PINEAPPLE (drained)
25 MARSHMALLOWS (finely-cut)
½ cup WALNUTS (chopped)
1 cup non-dairy WHIPPED TOPPING
1½ to 2 cups GRAHAM CRACKER CRUMBS
8 MARASCHINO CHERRIES

Combine first three ingredients and mix well. Let stand for one hour. Fold in whipped topping and chill for two hours. Form balls and roll in crumbs. Top each ball with a cherry. Chill for one hour before serving.

Loaf Style: This may also be placed in a loaf pan if you prefer. Mix ingredients as shown but use just one cup of crumbs. Place half of crumbs in the loaf pan and (instead of making balls) spoon mixture into pan and cover with rest of crumbs. Top with cherries and chill well before serving.

Orange-Applesauce Jell-O

1½ cups WATER
1 pkg (0.3-oz.) sugar free ORANGE JELL-O
½ cup APPLESAUCE
1 cup non-dairy WHIPPED TOPPING

Boil one cup water and dissolve Jell-O. Add rest of water and mix well. Refrigerate Jell-O until slightly thickened. Fold in applesauce and whipped topping and refrigerate until completely set.

Poor Man's Cake

1 Tbsp. MARGARINE
½ cup SUGAR
1 EGG (slightly-beaten)
½ cup MILK (fresh or canned)
1 cup FLOUR
1 tsp. BAKING POWDER
½ cup RAISINS (or chopped dates)

Cream margarine into sugar. Add egg and milk and mix well. Combine flour, baking powder and raisins and add to batter. Mix thoroughly. Bake in a greased 8-inch square pan at 350 degrees for 30 minutes, or until toothpick inserted into the middle comes out clean. Serve hot or cold with Lemon Sauce.*

*LEMON SAUCE

½ cup MARGARINE
1 EGG (beaten)
1 cup SUGAR
3 Tbsp. WATER
1 LEMON (juice and gratings)

Melt margarine and let cool. Beat in egg, sugar and water. Heat over low flame and bring to a slow boil, stirring constantly. Continue to cook and stir until mixture thickens. Add lemon juice and gratings. Stir and cook until well blended. Serve hot over cake or bread pudding.

BRANDY OR RUM SAUCE

Cook as directed above, but omit lemon and add 1 to 1½ jiggers brandy or rum. This sauce is delicious served with baked apples or over slices of fruit cake.

Cherry Vanilla Cake

1 POUND CAKE (sliced)
1 pkg. (6-serving size) VANILLA INSTANT PUDDING
1 can (1-lb., 9-oz.) CHERRY PIE FILLING
WHIPPED TOPPING (optional)

Place cake slices in bottom of greased baking pan. Prepare pudding according to instructions and spread over cake slices. Spoon on pie filling and spread carefully over pudding. Frost with topping or serve plain. Refrigerate until well chilled before serving.

Cherry Angel Cake Squares

1 loaf ANGEL FOOD CAKE
1 can (1-lb., 9-oz.) CHERRY PIE FILLING
1 carton (8-oz.) non-dairy WHIPPED TOPPING

Slice cake into one-half-inch thick slices and line bottom of 8- or 9-inch square pan with the slices. Cover with one-half of pie mix. Press mix into the cake with back of a spoon. Cover pie mix with rest of cake. Mix remainder of filling with 1½ cups of the whipped topping and spread that over the cake slices. Cover and refrigerate until well chilled. Serve with a spoonful of topping if desired.

Caramel Apple Cake

1 loaf ANGEL FOOD CAKE
1 pkg. (4-serving size)
   INSTANT BUTTERSCOTCH PUDDING
1 can (1-lb., 9-oz.) APPLE PIE FILLING
1 jar (10-oz.) CARAMEL ICE CREAM TOPPING

Slice cake into one-half-inch thick pieces and place in bottom of 8-inch square pan. Prepare pudding according to instructions and spread evenly over cake. Spoon on pie filling. Place open jar of caramel topping in a pan of hot water until warm enough to pour easily and drizzle over pie filling. Cover and chill before serving.

Butterscotch Pudding

1½ cups BROWN SUGAR (packed)
¼ cup FLOUR
2 EGGS (beaten)
1½ cups evaporated MILK

Combine sugar and flour in saucepan and mix well. Add other ingredients in order and mix thoroughly. Cook over medium heat, stirring constantly until pudding thickens (5 to 10 minutes). Chill before serving. (4 to 6 servings)

Mock Jelly Roll

1 pkg. (3-oz.) CREAM CHEESE
½ cup RASPBERRY JAM (or strawberry)
4 SPONGE CAKE CUPS (The little cakes used for
        strawberry shortcake)
1 to 1½ cups non-dairy WHIPPED TOPPING

Cream cheese and jam together. Place one-quarter of mixture in each cake cup. Frost with topping and serve chilled.

Applesauce Bread Pudding

4 cups BREAD CRUMBS
2/3 cup MILK (fresh or canned)
2 EGGS (beaten)
2 Tbsp. MARGARINE (melted)
1½ cups APPLESAUCE
¼ cup BROWN SUGAR
1 tsp. CINNAMON
½ cup RAISINS (optional)

Combine ingredients in order and mix well. Bake in greased 8-inch square pan at 350 degrees for 45 minutes to one hour. Serve with Lemon or Brandy Sauce.

Easy Strawberry Trifle

1 POUND CAKE
¾ cup STRAWBERRY JAM
1/3 cup ORANGE JUICE
2 to 3 Tbsp. SHERRY (optional)
¼ cup ALMONDS (sliced)
1 pkg. (4-serving size) INSTANT VANILLA PUDDING
1½ cups MILK
1 cup non-dairy WHIPPED TOPPING

Slice cake and place in bottom of 8-inch square pan. Use all of cake. Combine jam, orange juice and sherry and mix well. Pour over cake slices. Sprinkle with almonds. Prepare pudding with 1½ cups milk. Beat until thick and fold into whipped topping. Spread over cake and refrigerate until well chilled.

Baked Apple Custard Pudding

1 can (1-lb., 9-oz.) APPLE PIE FILLING
1½ cups soft BREAD CRUMBS
1 cup evaporated MILK
2 EGGS (beaten)
1/3 cup SUGAR
1 tsp. CINNAMON
½ tsp. SALT

Combine all ingredients and mix well. Pour into a greased baking pan (8-inch square). Bake at 350 degrees for 40 minutes, or until knife inserted in middle comes out clean. Serve with or without Nutmeg Sauce.*

*NUTMEG SAUCE

1 cup SUGAR
2 tsp. NUTMEG
2 Tbsp. CORNSTARCH
1 cup canned MILK (evaporated)
1 cup WATER

Combine first three ingredients in a saucepan and mix well. Gradually stir in milk and water. Cook over medium heat stirring continuously as sauce thickens. Serve hot.

Easy Fruit-Nut Crisp

1 can (1-lb., 9-oz.) PIE FILLING (cherry, apple or berry)
¼ cup BROWN SUGAR (packed)
3 Tbsp. MARGARINE
½ cup FLOUR
½ tsp. BAKING POWDER
½ cup WALNUTS (or pecans, finely-chopped)

Pour pie filling into a greased casserole. Combine rest of ingredients, in order, in a bowl and mix until well blended and crumbly. Sprinkle over pie filling. Bake at 350 degrees for 30 minutes, or until top is brown and filling is bubbly. Serve hot with heavy cream or ice cream or plain.

Soft Chocolate Frosting

½ cup SUGAR
3 Tbsp. COCOA
2 Tbsp. FLOUR
2/3 cup evaporated MILK (small can)
1 Tbsp. MARGARINE

Combine first three ingredients in small pan and mix well. Stir in milk and mix until smooth. Add margarine and cook over medium heat, stirring constantly as frosting thickens. It will have a pudding-like consistency. (Recipe frosts an 8-inch square cake.)

Fudge Brownie Squares

2 EGGS
1 cup SUGAR
6 Tbsp. COCOA
½ cup MARGARINE
¾ cup FLOUR
¼ tsp SODA
½ tsp. BAKING POWDER
1 tsp. VANILLA
½ cup WALNUTS (chopped)

Beat eggs and sugar together. Melt margarine and cocoa in a pan and mix well. Beat cocoa mixture into eggs and sugar. Add rest of ingredients and mix well. Pour into eight-inch square greased pan and bake at 350 degrees for 35 minutes. Cool and frost.

Campfire Cooking

Elaborate campfire cookery or hot dogs—anything tastes good around the campfire!

Campfire cooking is easy and fun if you have the proper tools. Because of limited storage space, most travelers are not able to carry a complete set of cookware for indoor cooking and another set for outdoor cooking. If you plan to cook some of your meals outside, we suggest you consider the following equipment:

- 10- or 12-inch CAST IRON SKILLET with cover
- 2- or 3-quart CAST IRON POT with cover
- pair of long TONGS
- pair of hot pad MITTS
- ROASTING STICKS (for hot dogs, marshmallows, etc.)
- Heavy duty ALUMINUM FOIL
- Plastic SQUEEZE BOTTLE for water in case of fire flare-ups.

Cast iron is heavy but nothing works better over a campfire. When cleaning it, be sure to dry thoroughly. A light coat of cooking oil will help keep it from rusting. I made sacks from light weight toweling for storing my campfire pans. If all of your cooking is done over the campfire, you will need a coffee pot or a kettle for heating water and another pot or a Dutch oven.

Many of our parks and forests have campgrounds with fire pits or built-in barbecues. You need to be sure fires are allowed in the area you plan to visit. The Park or Forest Services will give you all the information you need.

Camping equipment stores have a variety of outdoor tools available: roasting forks, popcorn poppers, barbecues that fold up for easy storage, folding ovens for the campfire or portable gas stoves and many other handy items.

We always carry a fire pan and a folding grill as there are some campgrounds without grills over their fire pits. If you are going to build your own fire pit, a grill is a necessity.

Build your own pit (if fires are allowed) by clearing leaves, twigs and rubble from a four-to-six-foot square area. Make a slight indentation in the middle of the cleared square and surround the indentation with large rocks. Place four small rocks in the pit, spaced properly to hold your grill up out of the coals.

When you prepare your fire, start with dry leaves and twigs, criss-cross larger twigs and sticks on top of the smaller ones and have the largest pieces of wood on top of that. Put the logs on when the fire has a good start. Don't build a fire too big for you to control and always put your fire out when you are through with it. This can be done by covering the fire with dirt or sand.

Use a small shovel to push the dirt out of the way the next morning because the coals may stay hot through the night. If you will be using charcoal for cooking, don't forget the starter fluid, but be careful about using it around an open fire.

Try some of the recipes cooked in foil packets first or the grilled chicken or steak. They do not require extra pans. If you are already a campfire cook, I am sure you are aware that all of the stove-top recipes in this book may be cooked over a campfire and many of the recipes for the oven, may be baked in a Dutch oven.

Campfire Stuffed Squash

1 medium-size ACORN SQUASH
½ lb. BULK SAUSAGE
1 cup INSTANT STUFFING MIX
½ cup WATER (boiling)

Cut squash in half, the long way, and remove seeds. Brown sausage and drain off grease. Add stuffing mix and boiling water and mix well. Mound stuffing in the squash cavities. Wrap each squash half tightly in heavy aluminum foil. Roast in hot coals for 40 minutes to an hour, turning frequently. When done, squash will feel soft when pressed firmly with tongs or edge of a fork. (Serves 2)

Potato-Onion Bake

1 medium POTATO (scrubbed)
1 slice RAW ONION
½ Tbsp. MARGARINE

Cut potato in half the long way and sandwich back together with onion and margarine in the middle. Wrap tightly in foil and roast in hot coals for 45 minutes to an hour. Turn frequently. Potato is done if it feels soft when pressed firmly with tongs or edge of a fork. (Serves 1)

Grilled Corn on the Cob

Allow two ears of corn per serving. Soak corn in salt water for several hours. Carefully pull husk down and remove corn silk. Pull husk up around corn. If the husk is too loose, wind a strip of foil around the middle of the corn cob to hold husk together. Roast on grill for 15 to 20 minutes, turning two or three times.

Campfire Steaks

Brush steaks with marinade about one hour before grilling. Baste them often with Steak Marinade* as you grill them over hot coals. (Best on medium-rare, but cook meat to your taste.)

Marinade is excellent on London broil. Baste often as you grill and slice meat thin to serve.

*STEAK MARINADE

¼ cup WORCESTERSHIRE SAUCE
2 Tbsp. CATSUP
1 Tbsp. VINEGAR (or lemon juice)
1 Tbsp. OLIVE OIL
½ tsp. GROUND MUSTARD
¼ tsp. GARLIC POWDER

Combine all ingredients in a small jar and shake to mix. Marinade will keep several weeks when refrigerated. Recipe may be doubled.

Camper's Stew

1 pkg. (1-cup size) BEEF GRAVY MIX
1 lb. STEW MEAT (cut into bite-size pieces)
1 Tbsp. MEAT TENDERIZER
3 POTATOES (peeled and diced)
4 CARROTS (scraped & thinly sliced)
4 small whole WHITE ONIONS (peeled)
1 tsp. CELERY SEED
1 tsp. PEPPER

Prepare gravy according to instructions on the package. Sprinkle meat with tenderizer. Divide meat and vegetables into four servings on individual sheets of heavy aluminum foil (about 12"x14"). Place meat and vegetables so packets will be as flat as possible. Add one-fourth of gravy, celery seed and pepper and fold foil up to make a double fold down the center of each pouch. Fold up ends in a double fold. Roast over coals for 1 to 1½ hours. Turn often, using tongs. Serve in the packets by placing packet on a plate and pulling foil open. Watch out for the hot steam!

Campfire Chili Stew

1 can (12-oz.) ROAST BEEF & GRAVY
1 can (16-oz.) WHOLE POTATOES (drained)
1 can (4-oz.) WHOLE MUSHROOMS (drained)
1 can (16-oz.) STEWED TOMATOES
1 tsp. CELERY FLAKES
1½ Tbsp. CHILI POWDER

Divide meat, potatoes and mushrooms into three or four servings on individual pieces of aluminum foil (about 12"x12"). Mix tomatoes with the rest of the ingredients and divide that over the packets. Fold foil, double seams down the middle and ends. Roast over coals for 15 minutes or until hot through.

Grilled Ham

1 one-pound canned HAM

Grill whole ham over fire for 15 minutes on each side. Use tongs to turn so that ham will not break apart. Baste often with Steak Marinade*, Orange Sauce* or Barbecue Sauce.*

Campfire Ham & Bean Bake

1 can (16-oz.) STEWED TOMATOES
1 can (8-oz.) TOMATO SAUCE
2 Tbsp. DRIED ONION (minced or chopped)
1 Tbsp. CHILI POWDER
1 tsp. CELERY FLAKES
¼ cup BROWN SUGAR (packed)
1 one-pound canned HAM (cut in bite-size pieces)
1 can (16-oz.) LIMA BEANS (drained)
1 can (16-oz.) BUTTERBEANS (drained)

In outdoor cooking pot, combine ingredients in order given. Stir to mix and cover (use foil if pot doesn't have a cover). Cook for one hour, stirring occasionally. (Serves 4 to 6)

Dog-Gone Good Hot Dogs

2 HOT DOGS (per person)
Raw ONION SLICES (1 per hot dog)
MUSTARD (or CATSUP)
BACON STRIPS (1 per hot dog)

Split hot dogs horizontally (not all the way through) to form a pocket. Put a thin slice of onion in each pocket along with a dab of catsup or mustard. Tightly wind bacon around hot dog to hold pocket closed. Secure bacon with a toothpick or a skewer. Roast over coals until bacon is crisp. Remove toothpick or skewer and serve on a bun.
Variation: Put a small slice of cheese in the pocket and then wind bacon or spread buns with a soft cheese spread.

Ham on a Stick

1 one-pound HAM
2 to 3 Tbsp. WORCESTERSHIRE SAUCE

Cut ham into four chunks. Brush each piece generously with Worcestershire Sauce. Place securely on a roasting fork or stick and roast over campfire. (Serves 4)

Grilled Chicken with Orange Sauce

1 2-lb. FRYER

A two-pound fryer will serve two. Split chicken in half. Grill over fire for 15 minutes on each side. Baste with Orange Sauce* and continue grilling until done. Baste often with sauce and turn several times.

*Orange Sauce

1 cup ORANGE MARMALADE
2 Tbsp. SOY SAUCE
¼ cup WATER
1 tsp. CORNSTARCH

Combine all ingredients in a saucepan and stir as marmalade melts and sauce thickens. If it gets too thick, add water a spoonful at a time until you reach desired consistency. Best when like thick syrup.

Potatoes in a Pouch

1 small-to-medium POTATO (scrubbed)
½ Tbsp. MARGARINE
1 slice (¾-oz.) PROCESSED CHEESE
PAPRIKA

Slice or dice potatoes onto a piece of aluminum foil (about 10"x12"). Dot with margarine, lay cheese slice on top and sprinkle with paprika. Place potatoes in a single layer. Fold foil up and make a double seam down the middle of the packet. Fold ends up double. Roast on coals, turning frequently with tongs, for about 45 minutes. Serve in the pouch. (Serves 1)

Barbecue Fish
(Chinese Style)

This recipe is for fish large enough to be cut into 1 to 1½-inch thick steaks. We use 10 to 15 lbs. dorado or yellow-fin tuna. Clean the fish, trim off fins, head and tail. Do not remove skin or scales. Using a sharp knife, slice fish steaks as shown in the illustration.

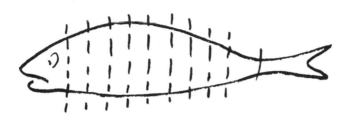

Place fish steaks in a shallow container that has a cover. A 9-inch square container holds about nine fish steaks. Pour marinade over fish.

Cover and refrigerate for two to four hours. If marinade does not cover fish, turn fish halfway through marinade time.

Grill fish over hot coals, basting frequently with Barbecue Fish Marinade.* Cooking time is about 30 minutes on each side. Meat will flake when tested with a fork when fish is done.

*BARBECUE FISH MARINADE

    1¼ cups SOY SAUCE
    1 LEMON (or 3 or 4 small Mexican limes)
    ½ cup WHITE WINE
    1 tsp. POWDERED GINGER
    ¼ tsp. GARLIC POWDER
    2 Tbsp. SUGAR

Pour soy sauce in a pint jar. Squeeze and grate lemon into it. Add rest of ingredients and shake to mix. Use for barbecued fish.

Lemon Trout

1 to 2 pan-size TROUT (per person)
LEMON SLICES
Raw ONION SLICES
MARGARINE
PEPPER
SOY SAUCE

Clean and trim trout. Leave whole with skin on (remove head if you prefer). Wash and dry fish. Place one lemon slice, one onion slice and one teaspoon margarine in body cavity of each fish. Place each fish on a piece of foil large enough to wrap it in. Sprinkle fish with pepper and one tablespoon soy sauce. Wrap each fish tightly in foil. Roast over fire about 15 minutes on each side. Fish will flake when done. Actual cooking time is determined by size of fish and hotness of fire.

(Do not cook several fish in one package. They don't seem to cook properly.)

Grilled Fresh Fish

1½ to 2-lb. FISH (per person)
MARGARINE
WHITE WINE

Clean fish, but do not scale or skin. Slice part way through body cavity toward back bone. Open fish butterfly fashion. Place over hot coals, skin side down. Dot each fish with margarine and sprinkle with about one tablespoon wine. Grill without turning until fish turns white and flakes when tested with a fork. Serve with slices of lemon or hot sauce.

Campfire Tuna Sandwiches

1 can (9¼-oz.) TUNA (drained)
1 Tbsp. SWEET PICKLE RELISH
3 Tbsp. soft processed CHEESE SPREAD
¼ cup MAYONNAISE
6 Hamburger BUNS

Flake tuna into a bowl. Mix in all of ingredients except buns. Mix well. Spread tuna mixture on buns and wrap each sandwich in foil. Cook over campfire five to eight minutes on each side.

Butter-Rum Roasted Apple

4 APPLES
1 jar (about 10-oz.) BUTTERSCOTCH
   ICE CREAM TOPPING
2 to 3 Tbsp. RUM
½ cup RAISINS (or chopped nuts)

Roast apples on a stick over the campfire. Combine topping, rum and raisins in a small pan and heat. Place roasted apple in a bowl and add two or three tablespoons of the sauce.

Roasted Caramel Apple

4 APPLES
1 jar (about 10-oz.) CARAMEL ICE CREAM TOPPING
½ cup WALNUTS (or peanuts, chopped)

Roast apple on a stick over the campfire. Heat topping by placing OPEN jar in hot water. Place roasted apple in a bowl, add two to three tablespoons topping and a sprinkle of nuts. So good you'll be tempted to eat the core! (Serves 4)

Campfire Cookies

Snappys

    1 bag MARSHMALLOWS
    1 bag GINGER SNAP COOKIES

Toast marshmallows and sandwich between ginger snaps.

Peanut Butter Surprise

    1 bag MARSHMALLOWS
    1 box VANILLA WAFER COOKIES
    1 jar PEANUT BUTTER (creamy or chunky)

Toast marshmallows and sandwich between vanilla wafers that have been spread with peanut bttter.

Fudgy Graham Crackers

    1 box GRAHAM CRACKERS
    1 can CHOCOLATE FUDGE FROSTING
    1 bag MARSHMALLOWS

Spread graham crackers with frosting. Toast marshmallows and sandwich between crackers.

Index of Recipes

Recipe Notes

Recipe Notes

ORDER BLANK

Golden West Publishers

4113 N. Longview Ave.   Phoenix, AZ 85014

Please ship the following books:

Number of Copies		Per Copy	AMOUNT.
	Apple-Lovers' Cook Book	5.00	
	Arizona Cook Book	5.00	
	California Favorites Cook Book	3.50	
	Chili-Lovers' Cook Book	5.00	
	Citrus Recipes	3.50	
	Cook's Book, The	5.00	
	Cowboy Cartoon Cook Book	5.00	
	Easy Recipes for the Traveling Cook	5.00	
	Easy Recipes for Wild Game & Fish	6.50	
	Joy of Muffins	5.00	
	Mexican Desserts	6.50	
	Mexican Family Favorites Cook Book	5.00	
	New Mexico Cook Book	5.00	
	Pecan-Lovers' Cook Book	5.00	
	Sphinx Ranch Date Recipes	5.00	
Add $1.50 to total order for shipping & handling			$1.50

Check (or money order) enclosed . . . $_____

Name _____

Address _____

City _____ State _____ Zip _____

This order blank may be photo-copied.

COOK BOOKS

Tempting recipes for luscious pies, dazzling desserts, sunshine salads, novelty meat and seafood dishes! Plus tangy thirst-quenchers with oranges, grapefruit, lemons, limes, tangerines, etc.
Citrus Recipes from the Citrus Belt by Al and Mildred Fischer (128 pages) ...$3.50

There's more to pecans than pecan pie! Indulge your pecan passion with recipes for pralines, macaroons, ice cream, bread pudding, torte, rolls, muffins, cakes and cookies, casseroles, nippy appetizers, hearty main dishes and, of course, a variety of tantalizing pecan pies!
Pecan Lovers' Cook Book by Mark Blazek (120 pages)...$5.00

Enjoy the versatility of dates in these tempting recipes for breads, puddings, cakes, candies, fruitcakes, waffles, pies and a myriad of other fantastic taste treats.
It's all in the **Sphinx Ranch Date Recipes** by Rick Heetland (128 pages)...$5.00

Great recipes, yet easy-to-fix, by hunter-traveler cook Ferne Holmes. Large game animals, small game, wild fowl, fish, side dishes, too! More than 200 recipes, fully indexed.
Easy Recipes for Wild Game by Ferne Holmes (160 pages). . .$6.50

COOK BOOKS

A taste of the Old Southwest, from sizzling Indian fry bread to prickly pear marmalade, from sourdough biscuits to refried beans, from beef jerky to cactus candy.

Arizona Cook Book by Al and Mildred Fischer (144 pages)...$5.00. *More than 210,000 copies sold!*

More than 250 easy-to-follow home-style favorite family recipes for tacos, tamales, menudo, enchiladas, burros, salsas, frijoles, chile relleno, carne seca, guacamole and sweet treats!

Mexican Family Favorites Cook Book by Maria Teresa Bermudez (144 pages)...$5.00

Chili cookoff prize-winning recipes and regional favorites! The best of chili cookery, from mild to fiery, with and without beans. Plus a variety of taste-tempting foods made with chile peppers.

Chili-Lovers' Cook Book by Al and Mildred Fischer (128 pages)...$5.00. *More than 110,000 copies sold!*

Treat yourself to the California lifestyle with this cornucopia of 400 recipes for avocados, citrus, dates, figs, nuts, raisins, Spanish and Mexican dishes, wines, salads and seafoods.

California Favorites Cook Book by Al and Mildred Fischer (144 pages)...$3.50

Recipe Notes

_____
_____
_____
_____
_____
_____
_____
_____
_____
_____
_____
_____
_____
_____
_____
_____
_____
_____
_____
_____
_____
_____
_____
_____